Corpus II

⟩

John D. Caputo, *series editor*

PERSPECTIVES IN
CONTINENTAL
PHILOSOPHY

JEAN-LUC NANCY

Corpus II
Writings on Sexuality

TRANSLATED BY ANNE O'BYRNE

FORDHAM UNIVERSITY PRESS
New York ■ 2013

Copyright © 2013 Fordham University Press

"The 'There Is' of Sexual Relation" appeared in French as *L'"il y a" du rapport sexuel*, © 2001 Editions Galilée, Paris. "The Birth of Breasts" and "Paean to Aphrodite" translate the augmented versions of these essays that appeared in French in *La naissance des seins, suivi de Péan pour Aphrodite* © 2006, Editions Galilée, Paris. The first French version of the former essay was published in 1996 by the École régionale des Beaux-Arts de Valence; the first French version of the latter appeared in *Le poids d'une pensée* (Montreal: Le Griffon d'argile/PUG, 1991).

This work has been published with the assistance of the French Ministry of Culture—National Center for the book.

Ouvrage publié avec le concours du Ministère français chargé de la culture—Centre National du Livre.

Library of Congress Cataloging-in-Publication Data

Nancy, Jean-Luc.
    [Il y a du rapport sexuel. English]
    Corpus II : writings on sexuality / Jean-Luc Nancy ; translated by Anne O'Byrne.
        pages cm.— (Perspectives in continental philosophy)
    Includes bibliographical references.
    ISBN 978-0-8232-4002-9 (cloth : alk. paper)
    ISBN 978-0-8232-4003-6 (pbk. : alk. paper)
    ISBN 978-0-8232-5204-6 (pdf)
    1. Sexual intercourse—Philosophy.   2. Sex—Philosophy.   3. Sex customs—History.   4. Man-woman relationships.   I. Title.
HQ12.N3613   2013
306.7—dc23

                                                                    2013027073

Printed in the United States of America
15 14 13   5 4 3 2 1
First Edition

Contents

Translator's Foreword

Jean-Luc Nancy has included many quotations in this text, particularly in "The Birth of Breasts." Where possible I have used existing published English translations from the original languages, occasionally adapting the translation to reflect an emphasis in the French text. Where the original is in French or German and I have not been able to identify an acceptable English translation, I have translated the piece myself. The one substantial exception is the long quotation from Theodor Lipps in "The Birth of Breasts," which is a translation of Nancy's translation. In a few cases where the original language is other than French or German, and I have not been able to locate either the original or an existing English translation, I have resorted to the thoroughly unsatisfactory solution of translating the French translation. These cases are identified in the accompanying footnotes.

I am grateful to all the following for their help with this translation: Lisa Archer, Michael Archer, Michael Beck, Patrick Burns, Lori Gallegos de Castillo, Robert Harvey, Ben Hett, Travis Holloway, Lee Miller, Virginie Palette, Michael Popowits, Alva MacSherry, Sarah Kindness, and Mary Rawlinson. I would also like to thank the New York Public Library for the use of its space and resources.

Corpus II

The "There Is" of Sexual Relation

Lacan tells us that psychoanalysis is founded on this principle: "There is no sexual relation."[1] Its corollary, or another formulation of the same principle, goes like this: "Jouissance is impossible."[2]

What interests me is not a further investigation of the ins and outs, or indeed the various transformations, of these statements of the principles, the very matrix, of the structure of psychoanalytic theory. I have neither the theoretical nor the clinical competence for that. Nor do I have the slightest intention to develop something or other from within that structure, just as I am not going to offer any proper commentary on the texts where it is all laid out. I am approaching it from the outside—I ask you to remember this—and I am interested above all in the way in which these statements are stated. In a certain sense, I could say that my starting point is what there is of stating in these statements, in all statements. Or perhaps the starting point is what is performative and pragmatic (in the linguistic sense) in these constative phrases. (They do present themselves as constative, as the affirmation of facts, albeit not as empirical facts but as what is given by the structure. The problem here is the relation between the empirical and the structure, between de facto relation and relation that de jure cannot be.) I start from what makes itself heard to me, from my hearing, which is certainly not analytic but which for that very reason has a certain way of floating, allowing resonances to emerge for me that will not harmonize with the unison of the Lacanian program. Rather, what I hear will sound against it, in contact with it, that is to say, as close to it as can be, but maybe also at the same time as far away as possible, in a sort of inverted echo, or maybe according to a relation (sexual? not sexual?) that is itself incommensurable. What am I being made to hear and understand? To what am I being asked to lend an ear? Toward what, to which side must I turn this ear?

Here it is a matter of stating a certain provocation, one founded on a paradox. We are stating that something that happens every day is not. (At least, there are "sexual relations" every day and, even as far as jouissance is concerned, it might not be as easy as we might wish to claim that it does not happen every day.) What is stated functions as a spectacular and quite astonishing announcement: What is, is not! A well-informed philosopher would point out right away that this is no more than obvious, since Hegel or Heidegger, each in a different mode, states that being is not. Yet these statements do not announce the non-existence of what exists; they say that "being," or the concept going by the name "being" that we take to be a verbal copula (note in passing that here we are, suddenly, in the midst of a copulation of some sort), or the action of what *being* is in the active sense (these two hypotheses overlap), cannot consist in some *thing* (not a pebble or God or flower or penis). Finally, they say that "being" is not something, but that "being" is this: that there are things in general. And that the "there is," the *fact* that there is (empirically and transcendentally all at once, in a single double stroke), or simply the "there is" itself, is no kind of being at all.

Does the same hold for sexual relation, which is not? In a certain way this may be the whole question. It is not impossible that in the end we will discover that "the sexual relation" behaves like "being" [*l'être*] (understood as verb and act) in relation to what will therefore be "being" [*étant*] for it (that is, the entwined couple). Or, if you like, what couples the couple is not a couple, without, for all that, being single either. What couples and therefore what "is" in the transitive sense that Heidegger requires—what moves being along, what traverses it and transports it, what ravishes it and what is ravished, that is, what inflames and exceeds it at the same time, in the same stroke—is neither one nor two nor, indeed, anything that can be counted.

Moreover, in the domain where we now find ourselves there is a word that functions as a verb and a noun: the word *baiser*, which we can appeal to as a noun ("a kiss") and as a verb ("to fuck") thanks to how it is used in slang (which has revived its classical meaning *donner un baiser* [to give (someone) a fuck]). You could say that "kiss" or "fuck" is not any existing kiss or fuck, given and received, but "kiss" or "to fuck" is the gift of fucking (where the giving and the receiving remain to be sorted out, though that would mean sorting out sharing itself, and it feels as though that would be absolutely tactless as regards the very touch, or the mouth, of the kiss). Meanwhile, what is expressed by the foundational expression of psychoanalysis is that I am kissed every time I kiss, fucked every time I fuck. (I don't know if Lacan took advantage of this resource, but I think it would be to his liking.) And the other, slang meaning of the verb could be testimony to what common knowledge conceives of in the sexual relation as a sort of trickery. Lacan carries this to the height of analytic knowledge, much as Kant does with common knowledge about the good will.

However, we should note that the pejorative sense of "fuck" (and, therefore, what is supposed to be common knowledge) refers to an etymology of the word that associates it with the category of having: one is had, one has been possessed (and, more particularly, buggered). This sense depends on a representation of the act (I won't dwell here on the word *act*, which Lacan differentiates in relation to "relation," so to speak: we'll come back to this) as the appropriation and domination of one by the other. And this representation depends on a preestablished schema that distributes the values and roles of activity and passivity. We know all too well—ever since Kant and maybe even since Plato—how fragile this schema is and the degree to which "passivity" is entwined and bound up with "passive power" (*potentia passiva, dunamis tou pathein*) and with what is known as "passion." Merely mentioning this term opens up inexhaustible and abundant perspectives on the whole of philosophy, literature, and theology, a whole *pathos* that can never be reduced to a pathology. For psychoanalysis, particularly in its Lacanian version, wants to be or to do something altogether different from a medicine used to treat a pathology. Let's say that it wants the ethos of a pathos.

When I fuck, I'm fucked, but how are we to understand this? Who fucks whom, and what does it mean to fuck or to be fucked?

Let us return to the question of the being of relation (of this relation that "is not"), and of how it is expressed. What makes this a clear provocation has to do with the logic and semiology of the statement: we have to understand, despite our astonishment, that what is not is not the same thing as what we know full well takes place. However, I'm not neglecting a secondary aspect, which might be a secondary benefit for the one making the statement: astonishment allows for "interdiction." There is something about interdiction that resonates here, like interrupting the couple fucking (since we also have what I would call the reciprocal use of the verb). What is sketched out is a performative pragmatics of coitus interruptus. On that count, the only thing to be understood is the forbidden [*l'interdit*]. We know very well that this is what is at stake in the end (if we see the sexual relation against the background of the incest taboo). But we also know that, even if psychoanalysis talks about castration, it certainly doesn't want to be the castrator. We have to search in a different way and no doubt also, in the end, to ask in another way what it means to forbid, if not to interrupt and uncouple the coupled couple. An ethos of pathos presumes that the couple *forbids* itself its coupling according to some mode other than renunciation.

When we begin trying to understand (I'm still speaking from the outside, approaching the analytic statement from the outside), we discover that the provocation in relation to empirical experience (that is, to the fact that there is relation every day) quickly turns out not to be the essential point. It is possible only by means of another provocation or by means of a sort of forcing of language. "There is no relation" is said in the way one would say "there is no oil in the well." (You get the feeling that there is more to be got out of this metaphor of the well, but this is not the place to do it.) This assumes that "relation" is some thing. This is not immediately given in language. The word *relation* makes us think of an action, not a substance. It does not designate either a substance, a support, or an agent [*un suppôt*] (a *suppositum*) except in a derivative way, where it takes on the sense either of an "account" ("police report") or of the "result of a relation [*relation*]" ("peaceful relations" [*rapport harmonique*]). It is clear then that the meaning of the word has slipped from the act to a product. (It has even happened that the word refers—in the work of Littré—to the instrument that has, as a result, been named a protractor [*rapporteur*]; the object that allows us to calculate the result of any given putting into relation.)

But, as it happens, *relation* sensu stricto does not designate any thing. In addition, it so happens that the expression "sexual relation" is not the one we use to say the thing. Even an indiscrete reporter would say "they slept together" and not "they had relations" or "they had a relation," at least so long as this reporter was not a police investigator or a doctor. The expression is really medical, or juridico-medical. It is the strictly physical and physiological objectification of what we designate only using verbs (*to bed, to make love, to fuck*, etc. or indeed, as in Proust, to make *catleya*). The oldest senses of the word [*rapport*] have to do with "revenue," or "giving an account" or "narrative," "convention" or "conformity"; they are the names of things or qualities. It is in this register—so juridical and economic in origin—that later the expression "intimate relations" and then "sexual relation" appeared.

When we say that there is no sexual relation we could mean that there is no revenue, no account to be given, no conformity or fixed proportion for what happens when a couple couples. And, in fact, there is none of that. If it is a matter of the relation *of* or *to* the subject of the sexual act, of what this act *reports* or what can be *retained, retold, calculated,* or *capitalized* (and therefore inscribed or written in this sense), then we surely have to say that account, measure, or even general appropriation or determination of it as "some thing" is impossible. This relation cannot be counted or recounted (which is the whole problem of erotic literature). It can only be accounted for, as I have already indicated, in relation to—that is, from the given angle of or in the specific guise of—an understanding that is medical, physiological, or even psychological, that is, energetic and eventually also pathological and sociological, not forgetting the perspective of a possible conception (in which case, of course, we limit the angle to heterosexual relations without contraception, excluding all others, not least autoeroticism). That is to say, it can only be accounted for from the angle of a police or judicial or religious investigation.

If relation is pursued from the angle of a "something," we can say that there is no relation *of* the sexual, or that the sexual does not relate anything. Maybe this is what Lacan wants to indicate when he says that a relation writes itself and that the sexual does not write itself, by which we should understand that writing is a matter of consigning rather than signifying, a matter of a graph or algorithm rather than literature. Maybe the question is this: What is there of the sexual relation in all of literature, poetry in particular (but perhaps also—who knows?—in all of philosophy)? To talk of "sublimation" in a way that we can understand means knowing what is sublimated and what that operation consists in. After all, there is nothing to say that the structure or nature of what is supposed to be sublimated is not still in play, still acting within what we call sublimation.

By this path, and through the other gaps and avenues I have briefly suggested, we always come back to the same point: in the case of sexual relation there is no thing, nothing that would constitute the accomplishment of the sexual relation, its substance and entelechy. (This is an Aristotelian term that signifies only the final, completed state of some being or other, the point where its being is completed, perfected, which can also perhaps represent the point or the completion of being. In any case, for Aristotle, it is above all a matter of individual or completely individuated beings). For this is the point where the forcing of language that is in play in what is stated as much as in the statement must be our focus. It must be reactivated or excavated all over again

If the early senses of *relation* fell under the heading of what I would call *relation of*, the contemporary sense has much more to do with what must be called the *relation-between* (or even, if we want to stick more closely to what has gone before, the *relation of . . . to*). This is particularly the case in philosophy or, more broadly speaking, in the contemporary humanities. Relation designates very precisely that which is not the thing, which is not any thing (no substance, no entelechy), but which (if we can still say *which*, since in this case saying *this* or *which* has a value different from in the case of the thing) happens between things, from one thing to another. Maybe we can put it like this: relation [*rapport*] entwines itself again in the logical-philosophical register of *relation* [*relation*] in general. ([The French words] *relation* and *rapport*—two terms that come from verbs designating the act of carrying, transporting—are synonyms, though they have many other meanings too, but *relation*, which we mostly keep for referring to a love affair rather than copulation, places greater emphasis on dynamic, active possibilities, the possibilities of narrative).

Relation [*relation*] is one of the four classes into which Kant, in a parallel way, divides up judgments and categories.[3] The three divisions of this class are categorical judgment and the category of inherence and subsistence ("this belongs to that," "this is a property or an accident of that"), hypothetical judgment and the category of causality and dependence ("this causes that," "this is the effect of that"), and disjunctive judgment and the category of community or reciprocal action between actor and the sufferer of the action (the coordination of parties that are separate but which nevertheless act upon one another in a totality, as much by their disjunction as by their conjunction). The third category is obviously the one that gives the class of relation its wide range and comprehensiveness: the relations of inherence and causality could meet—but also could reciprocate or even return to their negation—in the register of community (or connection or coordination, to use other words of Kant's). The relation of reciprocal action is in a certain way relation absolutely considered. We can also attribute to it the sort of properties that would be provided by a logic of relations, for example, that the relation between two terms does not exist between two others, that the negation of a relation is still a relation, that every relation has a converse (or an inverse form), and so on for various other properties that a more complete knowledge could show us.

The important thing is that this logic of relation [*relation*] or relation [*rapport*] is not at all the same as a logic of substance or predicate (including the relation of predication). This distinction is found in what is known as an ontology of relation: relation is not a being, it takes place between beings. It is—insofar as it is, or according to the mode of being which is not precisely ipseity (let's say presence, being given, being put there)—it is of the order of what the Stoics called the incorporeal. They listed four instances of the incorporeal: space, time, the void, and the *lekton* (the said, the stated). As you see, these four instances of the incorporeal are the four instances or four conditions of relation: they in effect require a distinction between places, a difference between times (including what we know as simultaneity, for this is where two *tempi* are made synchronous or syncopated), an empty interval between bodies, and the possibility of the emission and reception of a saying—of an inter-saying, a saying between, or a bidding forth, a for-bidding. In fact, this last condition would appear to be optional, and it is, up to a point, but only to the point where we might have to grant that a relation, whatever it is, makes something like sense, even if that is initially simply directional sense (the relation of setting in motion), then sense-able sense (the relation of skin to the skin it touches, or of an eye to the color that delights it). Or that it caresses and then relates significance, which is both a direction (even if it must go in both directions) and a sensibility (because the saying touches and is in itself the register of the voice) that all the while produces signification, even if it is incomplete and uncompleteable and consists in the infinity of its referring from one to the other, that is, in relation insofar as it refuses conclusion and also refuses to allow its story to be told or related.

A relation is therefore always of the order of the fourfold incorporeal, which is also the fourfold condition of sense. We can take it up again here as the distinction between bodies. If bodies were not distinct from one another, they would not be bodies, just an undifferentiated, unformed mass. If they are distinct, it must be in the double sense of their being separate and the separation being what permits them to relate to one another. The one distinguishes the other in all senses: one perceives the other, chooses him, honors him. It follows that relation is not in any way a being: it is not anything distinct, but rather distinction itself. Or, more accurately, it is the *distinguishing oneself* in which the distinct comes into its own, and it does so only in relation to others, which are also distinct. In relating to itself the distinct distinguishes itself. That is to say, it opens and closes itself at the same time. It returns to the other and separates itself from it. Relation is only possible as part of this duel. I would like to invoke here both the grammatical value of the term in certain languages (Sanskrit and Greek, for example) and also the sense of single combat, but without drawing on any sense of singularity's numerical value. The two [parties] confront each other only in order to let something come to be in the empty space between them, something like an ordeal, a divine judgment where honor is in play, that is to say, precisely, the absolute distinction or the dignity of each. (Of course, we could replay certain themes here that have already often been interpreted in terms of the contest of love: the assault, the mingling, and the fact that, if not life, then at least existence or being in the world is at stake—Monteverdi's *Combatimento* and Hemingway's "little death.")

Therefore, it follows that relation happens only by means of distinction, and that it is—insofar as it is—what distinguishes beings (which I have here named bodies) without itself being. To say that there is no relation is then to state what is proper to relation: in order to be, it must not be a third thing between two. Rather, it must open the *between* as such: it must open the *between two* by means of which there are two. But what is between two is not either one of the two: it is the void—or space, or time (including, once again, simultaneous time), or sense—which relates without resembling, or resembles without uniting, or unites without finishing, or finishes without carrying to its end. (This is why the "without-relation" of relation has become an almost obsessive preoccupation for contemporary thought, to the point where this relation itself needs to be turned around: if without-relation opens relation, relation in turn clears the way for without-relation.)

The without-relation of relation, as the essence of relation (or, if we prefer, that which is relation insofar as there is no relation), is not a dialectical pirouette. It is its paradoxical reality as the thing (*res*, the real) of what is only between things. The great Scholastic knew this very well and attributed to relation or *relatio* a tiny modicum of being at the limit of being as a being [*à la limite de l'être en tant qu'étant*] (a *minus ens*). This is also why, in Aquinas, relation cannot be described as "substantial" (it is "accidental," that is, it is itself related to a substance or subject that it is not). The exception is the divine substance, which is *relatio* all by itself. That is to say, it is the relation that prevails between the three persons of the Trinity. Put another way, the relation between things presupposes the separation between subjects, and relation itself, understood as *res*, is equal to the being in itself outside itself of the uncreated. (Very many things flow from this regarding creation and the reason for creation in a divine love, but those can be examined elsewhere.) Put in still another way, on the one hand, the relation and separation between subjects (things or persons) are one and the same thing, while, on the other, this same thing is sameness itself as different from itself and deferring itself, or desiring itself, or loving itself, all of which is a single reality or a single movement that is as foreign to the logic of fulfilled identity as it is to the symmetrical logic of constitutive lack or separation.

This logic of relation could also be stated like this: it responds strictly to the other Lacanian axiom (maybe his Ur-axiom, the one that ties him so firmly to both Heidegger and Bataille) according to which there is no whole at all [*il n'y a pas de tout*]. (Woman "not whole" ["*pas-toute*"], with her knowledge of jouissance, is the emblem of this axiom.) But that there is no whole (or *the* whole) is not the definition of a lack or the indication that something has been taken away, because there was no whole before there was no whole-at-all. It indicates, rather, that all that there is (for there is indeed all that there is) does not totalize itself, even though it is the whole. Here, the whole must be heard: there is, in effect, the all of wholeness (*holon,* totum) and the all of all the wholes or of all the world or everyone (*pan, omnis*). Yet what is the all of a coupling couple? It is certainly not a whole. If it is a beast, it is the one with two backs. Two do not make one, but two thrusts, two impulses, a couple of forces are needed, and their interplay—distance in contact—keeps the machinery in motion. It is never a question of a support, at most a transport; relation supports itself by its transport alone.

Meanwhile, when we claim that there is or there is not, we must know *where* the *there* is. If we are speaking of some thing, it can be here or there, but if it is a matter of what is neither a thing nor a being, that is, when it is a matter of all things or the relation of things, the *there* is no place, no place for any sort of a unity, but only the spacing of taking place and the play of between-place.

By now you will have already translated everything I have just said about relation in general into sexual terms. But we must go further and be more precise. After all, the sexual relation—if we begin to understand it as what there is of the fact that it is not—does not constitute a species of relation in general. The categorial logic of relation cannot have the last word. The sexual is not a variety of the genre known as relation, but in the sexual we see the extent of relation and see it fully exposed. I could say that the sexual relates [*rapporte*] what there is of relation [*rapport*], but its report— its account and its narrative—is not totalizing and does not close the circle.

In fact, one cannot simply predicate *sexual* of *relation* [*rapport*] as one can predicate *medical* or *official* of *report* [*rapport*]. All that I have said makes this clear enough. The sexual is not a predicate, for it itself is no more a substance or a thing than relation is a substance or thing.[4] The sexual is its own difference, or its own distinction. Being distinguished as sex or as sexed is what makes sex or sexed-ness. This is also what makes the sexual relation possible and is not, finally, the taking place of its own entelechy. After all, no one is man or woman without remainder, just as no one is homo- or hetero-sexual without remainder (if we want to use these categories, as if the sexual were not, in all these figures, the reciprocal action of the homo- and hetero-, their being shared, shared out, and mingled).

Sex is not just its own difference but also, each time, the properly infinite process of its own differentiation. I am each time a certain degree of composition and differentiation between *man* and *woman, homosexual man* and *heterosexual man, homosexual woman* and *heterosexual woman* and according to the various combinations that open up to each other as well as close themselves off from each other, that touch and penetrate each other. These infinite combinations—since none of the terms is given, neither a terminus a quo nor a terminus ad quem—are simply what is known as the sexual relation. But this is a sharp reminder that we must avoid saying "the" sexual relation. We have to stop using a noun and instead turn to what verbs try to say: *to bed, to do, to fuck*, but also *to take, to penetrate, to jerk off, to touch*. They are all verbs that [in French] can be conjugated in the reflexive—*to fuck oneself, give oneself, touch oneself*— though without losing the necessary ambiguity of this reflexivity, which always moves back and forth between auto- and alloeroticism. For it is precisely here again, here above all, or for example, that it becomes a matter of distinguishing oneself, distinguishing a self, distinguishing it from the other, distinguishing it by the other, distinguishing it by distinguishing the other, distinguishing oneself with the other, that is, with and from the other. Everything that remains indistinct is accounted for by this *with*, this co- of the *community* or of *copulation*. Copulation is the *with* (co-) of a link, a liaison (*apula*, from *apio*), in the same way that coitus is the with of a going (*ire*), of a coming and going, the movement of which, the approach and retreat, the touch and withdrawal constitutes (or founds, structures, signifies, symbolizes, or activates, whichever you like) in a very precise way the co- itself, which is nothing in itself, nothing but relation, nothing but the shattering of the identical and the one-in-itself. In fact, this is just what sex does; it shatters the one-in-itself. But this "one" does not pre-exist sex. There is nothing, no one that subsists before sexuation or outside of it, and this is a separation and relation that cuts across every "one," originarily (it divides the origin), as it passes between individuals and shares, divides or structures groups. Besides, we should not forget that sexuation divides a great many animals and vegetables, and that there is sex in what we think we can call *nature*—which needs more than just a commentary but at the very least this: it is through sex that human technology activates nature by practicing selective reproduction or hybridization, which is the condition for what is known as *culture*. The sexual relation is also the principle of an indefinite proliferation of these differences.

Generally speaking, the non-unity and non-unicity of the one is the absolute condition for there being one. That is to say, one and the other, the one *singuli* (always in the plural) and not the one *unus*. Philosophy from Plato to Hegel has known that this *unus*, the one purely in itself (the only one, as we see from the etymology of the word) is its own negation insofar as it relates immediately to itself. This also signifies that the immediate relation to oneself is at one and the same time the negation of the one, the self, and the relation, whether the relation to oneself or the relation to the other. The one excludes itself from itself, as Hegel put it.[5] As a result, if we want to speak of relation (of every sort of relation) in terms of *union*, we must once again consider that union cannot make one without immediately suppressing it.

But if the one excludes itself from itself, twos (and not "the" two) do not consist in two "ones" any more than they are two moments, two figures, or two remainders of one preexisting "One." Rather, duality includes itself in itself; it repeats itself. It divides itself (hetero/homo, masculine/feminine, etc.), it rejoices in itself (each time first and last, each time experiencing jouissance in being infinitely finite), and it also presents itself (love in art, love as art, and the relation between the two, which is a huge field of study).

The difference of the sexes is not the difference between two or several things, each one existing for itself as "one" (*a* sex): it is not like a difference between species or between individuals, or a difference of nature or degree. It is the difference *of* sex as differing from itself. For every living sexual being and in all regards, sex is the being's differing from itself, differing understood as differentiating itself according to multiple measures and according to all those tangled processes that go by the names *masculine/feminine, homo/hetero, active/passive,* and so on, and differing understood as the species multiplying indefinitely the singularities of its "representatives."

That is to say, there is no difference of the sexes, but there is, first and always, sex differing and deferring itself. And sex differing and deferring itself must be thought simply as relation, that is, not as being in relation to this or that (for example, in relation to another sex) but as relation itself, that is, as "relating oneself," that is, once again, the opening between of the *between* itself, of the "between ourselves," of intimacy. Sex differing and deferring itself is the spacing of intimacy.

Intimacy is the superlative of interiority (*interior intimo meo*: perhaps the whole history of sex in the West has to do with this Augustinian god who is so intimate with the subject). What interiority is shared and shared out sexually? Precisely not the interiority of any given identity, nor of any relation to self [*rapport à soi*], that is, of any relation in itself [*rapport en soi*]. What is shared and shared out and what is spaced out is precisely what does not exist for itself, for there is nothing—no generality or indifference or asexuality—that could ever underlie sex. There is nothing that could be before or outside spacing. Nothing could be before or outside the self-relation-to-sex that makes sex self-differing and self-deferring, and that, in this self-differing and deferring of sex,[6] may indeed create the very structure of what Lacan calls *the symbolic*. Is the *symbolon* not a sexed or sexing figure, one that requires putting together two pieces, coupling them? But primordial unity is precisely what is *not* behind this coupling, and the coupling does not produce anything like a final unity. If the one suppresses itself, it can neither split apart from itself nor be reunited with itself. Also, the couple is not the product of an indivisible unity without sex, nor does it fuse to produce a one that would be beyond the sexes.

There is no place, therefore, for supposing that something like an initial or a final unity must underlie division and separation. If we were to put this in the form of a constative (or contraceptive!) statement, it would be both an interdiction and an imperative: "jouissance is impossible!" Or maybe we have to understand *interdiction* in a completely new way. Maybe we have to hear what the word itself says: the diction or saying that is said *between*, not in this case to adjudicate a dispute (which was the sense of the Latin word), although this dimension is not absent (in the sense that it is a dispute, a debate, a trial undertaken for no reason other than its own undertaking), but in order to open up the *between* itself. For even if the sexual relation, or the self-relation of differing and differing oneself, is not written in the sense that Lacan proposes, it certainly is said. Not only is it spoken, sometimes with words of language—and what words other than the words of coming! [*jouir!*], words the first or the last of which might be "I am/you are coming!" [*je/tu jouis!*] a tautology in the form of an address, all of which deserves a long digression—but it is itself in fact nothing but a saying, though a saying whose sense is jouissance, not signification, which also surely indicates that significance in general is jouissance beyond all signification ("coming sense" ["*jouis-sens*"], as Lacan might have put it).

If the statement "jouissance is impossible" is a contraceptive as a constative, it is in the sense of not conceiving jouissance, which is to say, very precisely, in the sense of conceiving of it as inconceivable or conceiving of it without a concept. And what if *jouir* meant *to conceive without a concept* (to enjoy or to suffer [*pâtir*] in general)? Knowledge of jouissance, or knowledge of relation, is a matter of knowing exactly what is not an object of knowledge.[7]

Jouissance is not the jouissance *of* sex, as though it were some sort of good that could be possessed, and it is not jouissance *by* sex, as though it gave access to the possession of some good. In this context, using the language of subject and object is particularly dangerous, because it implies, at least in philosophical discourse, the constitution and representation of the object by and for the subject. But sex neither constitutes nor represents any such thing; it differs and defers *itself*, so it is neither its subject nor its object. Jouissance is the fact or the being of sex insofar as it differs and defers itself. The representation of a fusion, whether original or terminal, represents the extinction of jouissance. The whole history of eroticism testifies to this, from Plato to Henry Miller, not forgetting the troubadours along the way. The same history would also testify—if we wanted to pause here—that pleasure does not exist without touching on suffering, and the joy of anguish: this touch does not itself exist, as it should, without spacing and differentiation.

(In a more general way, it should be added that desire, properly speaking, has no object. What desire desires is not ob-jected by it, is not placed before it as though opposite it, but rather is part of its desiring movement. The thing of desire can no more be ob-jectified than it can be subjectified. It is not "-jectable" or "throw-able" at all. It is neither the lost object nor the subject of a quest but the throw itself or the throwing, the sending, the address, the inter-jection.)

We find the same testimony in Freud, so long as we make sure to separate out in his work the parts that remain determined by a model of opposition between excitation (so-called "preliminary" pleasure) and satisfaction (so-called "terminal" pleasure), and the parts that in certain regards exceed this scheme of tension and discharge, almost without Freud himself being aware of it. Pleasure happens in desire and as desire, thus conforming to the double sense of the German *Lust*, to which Freud refers (and which is also to be found in the Greek *eros* and the Sanskrit *kama*). When desire is satisfied, it is both its own extinction and its own excess: in discharging itself it also provides the incommensurable measure of an entropy that never takes place (except perhaps provisionally, and thanks to the impossibility of subsisting in a tension without end). Jouissance is precisely the simultaneity of release and the excess of tension. We could describe this as "impossible" if we wished, not in the sense in which we would have to acknowledge a fantasy of fusion as an impasse, but rather in the sense that the impasse in question is precisely what opens the way—to what? To the infinity of desire-pleasure, which is the infinity of sex deferring and differing itself. (And, if we need to be reminded again, desire-pleasure must also be noted as a certain dis-pleasure: beyond contentment.)

It is essential to determine with enough precision what we are talking about when we talk about "desire." We could stay within the scheme of privation where desire is a lack of being, and there is a whole tradition that puts it this way. In the Freudian lexicon we are then closer to *Wunsch* (that is, wish [*le souhait, le voeu*]) than *Gier, Begierde*, or *Gelüste*, which is empty ardor, *appetite* in its primary sense of tension and impulse. Moving from one register to another, we pass from a motion that is drawn out by absence and lack to an emotion that is excited by a presence that asks to assert itself again. This is how Descartes distinguishes between the desire to avoid what harms us (and therefore to recover a missing good) and the desire that comes from "some sort of titillation that . . . produces joy" and that desires "to find something that can enable us to continue in this joy, or else to have a similar joy again later on."[8]

But, all things considered, this duality of desire has been part of our eroticism since Plato. There it takes the form of the couple who are the parents of Eros: Penia, who is poverty or lack, and Poros, who is passage, with all his resourcefulness and his life impulse (the opposite of aporia or impasse).[9] We must think of Eros as the intimate connection between the two, and this requires, first of all, making sure that desire is not determined unilaterally by its Latin *etymon* (*desidero*, "to no longer see the stars, to find oneself in a state of lack, to be out of order"). Qualified in this way, desire is nothing but disaster, and a thinking that tries to make sense of it opens onto an ontology of loss—a dis-astrology or, if you prefer to stick with Greek, a catastrology. But if desire is double, lack is also the opening of its impulse and the thrust of its unreleaseable tension—a *consideration*. If there is a lack, it is the lack of nothing, that is, of no object because all is subject to it. The desiring subject can only relate to a subject that is itself a desiring subject. Of course, it is a subject that lacks its own substance and its own presupposition, because it is a subject ahead of itself, infinitely ahead of itself—a subject in surrection rather than in subsistence.

(I do not want to delay us, but I must add that the inevitable proximity, indeed intimacy, between Thanatos and Eros is in play here too. They are both ahead of the subject, and they both draw it on together, the one in the other, intimating one another. *To intimate*, command, prescribe comes from the same root as *intimate*: it is always pushed inside.)

The subject of desire is insatiable, not because it never reaches the point of being sated but because it does not respond to a logic, an economy, or an energetics of satiation. It feeds on itself, but this is not a matter of repletion or a return to self. It is, rather, a matter of an *intimation*, a pressing demand to always go deeper, to the innermost depths. What feeds on itself is also what opens relation. Hume analyzed the sexual relation as made up of three affections: first, the "appetite of generation," which does not relate directly to the generating (of new beings) but rather to genitality for, as he says, "sex is not only the object but also the cause of the appetite"; second, a "generous kindness or goodwill," which cannot but accompany—even if only momentarily—the act, as though what is generative [*le génésique*] were inherently generous; and third, the sensation or sentiment of beauty, which quickens or revives the appetite, for this sentiment of beauty is, Hume explains, nothing other than pleasure taken in "sympathy" (later it will be called "empathy") with a pleasure of the other in his own body.[10] The beauty of the body I desire is also what pleases that body itself. In this way, the relation between the sexes breaks down like a three-part polyphony, which each time concerns a pleasure or desire that tends toward itself even though its self-sameness consists in its alterity. For that very reason—because its identity consists in its difference—this relation can properly only be infinite, which means both interminable and entirely present each time it is in play.

The finitude of relation or jouissance (which is, after all, what Lacan wants to make us understand) must be understood as what punctuates (finishes, terminates, *and fines*, that is, refines) sexual infinity. This infinity is not the bad infinite of being condemned to constantly start poking around in the impasse all over again (note the double entendre that slang makes possible). It is the good infinite or the actual infinite—it is infinity in the actuality of the act itself insofar as it is the act of exceeding itself. Sex essentially exceeds itself, which is why it is essentially exciting. For to relate oneself, in the sense that I've said, is to excite oneself, to carry oneself outside, to spurt or spout out. Indeed, desire is not extinguished once it is satisfied; by reaching the point of discharge it exceeds itself again. Pleasure described as "terminal" is only the end of a sequence within a movement that is properly endless. Moreover, this pleasure exceeds pleasure identically: at the outer limits of a displeasure there is an exhaustion in the two senses of the word, almost a groan, a moan, sometimes a supplication.

We really should pause here to consider the matter of this other writing, the literature that is devoted to this pleasure. We should pause at the place occupied by love in literature and poetry. But I will limit myself to a brief citation from Celan, one that needs a far longer commentary: "The kiss, at night,/burns sense into a language." [11]

The "burning of sense," which is also the burning of the senses, each one taking place in or by the other, is what escapes representation. It cannot be understood as a form or a figure that leads to a ground, or a means destined to disappear into an end that is a presence without form, a fusion, absorption, or consummation. Certainly, the act "consummates itself" and consumes itself, but not in the form of entropic surfeit or in the symmetrical form of the gaping impossibility that lies beneath fantasy. The act consummates itself in not ending; it makes neither one nor two, it has no result, it never stops beginning, and it never stops finishing. In one sense it is confined to the simple sentiment—or simple shock—of existing itself, existing that, to be precise, is neither separate nor fused, for those are two ways of missing the true sense of the term *existing*.

The excitement that comes with the pleasure of tension is not "preliminary," as Freud put it. Or maybe it is preliminary in the sense that it precedes the threshold—the *limen*—at which it properly touches the intimacy of its own being excited. This is the logic of erogenous zones, the logic obeyed by the pleasure of tension as the tension of pleasure. Erogenous zones are nothing but the evidence, right at the body, of sex differing and deferring itself. Here the body is transcendental as empirical (or existential as existentiell). Its being divided up into zones is a division that is not a preestablished given. It has little to do with physiological divisions, but it does bring about sexual or sexing spacing. (I will leave aside for lack of time a consideration of the coincidence of genital zones and the reproductive function, the conjunction of the excess of jouissance and the excess of fertility, which is possible but not necessary.) Sex zones itself, if I can put it that way. It divides itself (*zonē* in Greek means "belt" in the sense of enclosure, separation, delimitation). The difference between one zone and another (from breast to belly to ear, from lips to armpits—but can we even name the zones using names that are already anatomized? the zones are zoning itself, they are the caress, and the kiss is a sort of caress) is a difference that is both nothing and absolute, a difference that is undifferentiable because it is differentiation itself, actual differentiation, and therefore in excess of all designation.

All by themselves the zones are worth nothing, as substances or organs. If they are organs, then they are organs of pleasure/desire, in other words, organs of an incorporeal body and not of any physiological body. Zones are valuable as the *eros* that they do not produce or contain but that they *are* insofar as they are excited (or allow themselves to be excited). Their value is the incalculable value of a self-differentiation and a self-exceeding. In the same way, it is impossible to calculate either the limits or the number of zones. As Freud has already said, the whole body can become erogenous. Zones are mobile and fleeting circumscriptions, identical to the gestures that designate them as zones and excite or inflame them. In this sense, there are as many zones as there are gestures, indefinitely repeated and modulated.

Of course, there are regions we might choose where genitality and therefore generation are tied up with eroticization. All this says is that the significance of the one need not be exhausted in the other: pleasure and the child might be two distinct figures of incalulable excess, but it might not be possible to superimpose one on the other. Maybe this is why they want to remain completely ignorant of one another: pleasure does want to see itself as the power of generation, and the child cannot recognize itself in the relation that produced it. In this sense, relation declares that there is no child, and the child declares that there is no relation. Each has to insist that there is no relation between them. It is a negation out of which both are composed. What is the mutual relation of the body of pleasure and the body of the child? The child's body could be understood as an erogenous zone that detaches itself and takes on an autonomous destiny. Between the body of pleasure and the child's body there is perhaps a communication of orifices, of what opens and absorbs or rejects the various elements—breath, humors, fluids, heat, tissues, tensions.

Could we say that the discourse of the body as zoned is an interpretation? But zoning and *eros* are just the self-interpretation of the body (that is, of the soul, if you prefer to give it that name). We would even have to say that sex essentially interprets itself. What I mean is that it performs itself, carries itself out, by sexing itself. It performs itself like a partition; it plays its own partition, the sharing and sharing out that there is of multiple sexes. The zoned body emblazons itself as the actual taking place of differing and deferring.

It is not a matter of denying either tension as such or the fact that tension cannot reach beyond the opposition between tension and détente to an intensity that eternalizes itself in presence to self. Of course we never reach this, but that is not the point. The point is precisely in the reaching insofar as it reaches nothing but itself. It is a reaching that is not a matter of gaining access so much as being a surprise [*une survenue, une surprise*] and therefore remaining essentially hidden from itself. One does not reach jouissance, for jouissance *is a reaching*. This is surely also what sets it in a fragile or painful proximity to a *crisis*, and to all that comes into play around it, if sex is not there. Sex can fail, it can fail to sex itself or exceed itself; otherwise, there is nothing at stake.

Let me add at this point that relation as zoning, that is, as the configuration of a body of relation (a body as the place of the sense of relation), begins and goes far beyond any strictly sexual occurrence. Freud himself describes how we take pleasure first in terms of sight, or hearing, and so on. By degrees we find that the sexual relation is in force wherever relation is in play, absolutely. That is to say, it is in force everywhere anything is put in play that could be called an *actual infinition* of two or more than two finite realities turning toward each other, opening to one another the intimacy of their infinity. There is perhaps no better definition of jouissance and relation than the *intimacy* of *infinity* and the *infinity* of *intimacy*.

What is surprising, then, in *intimate relations* is not that two intimacies are put into relation as if they were two given things, one on either side (as if I could have an intimacy *on my own behalf*, as they say, that is, *apart from the other*). On the contrary, what is surprising is relation itself as intimacy. But we must be sure to understand the proper nature of intimacy, which is that of the superlative, *intimus*, the most *intus*, the innermost. It is the inner such that there is no deeper or higher inner. But the depth in question has no ground: if there were a ground, somewhere it could be grounded or founded (in whatever sense), and it (or he or she) could not even enter into relation. This is because a ground assures and fixes a being on its proper substance. The intimate is always deeper than the deepest ground (which is also why it touches on the *extimate*, this term coined by Lacan—or perhaps I should say, the term he extimates . .). But the intimate is also the place of a sharing, both of oneself and of the other. This is what is demonstrated by the "intimate journal," the "secret diary." Yet is there any writing that is not in one way or another just such a journal?

If there is something impossible about jouissance, it is that there is intimacy, that is, there is a what (or a who) that recoils endlessly from every possible summons. The impossibility of jouissance means that it comes about only by not being deposed in a certain state (as in legal language, where one "enjoys a good") and that its result is its act itself. But it does happen, in this way. This is all it does. In this sense, jouissance knows nothing of the distinction between potential and actual. It is actual as potential, and this potentiality (which should not be confused with what is known as "sexual potency") is the very possibility of the impossible—passive potential as much as active potential. Jouissance enjoys itself, and this can happen only in the distinction, division, and relation of more than one who experiences jouissance. To say that jouissance enjoys itself is to say that it can be only as the other to itself, as what it is, not as "possible" in the sense of something that can happen or not happen, but "possible" in the sense that it contains—and liberates—the power of the impossible. Here, the difference between the sexes is intimacy itself, and for that reason can only with great difficulty be separated out into roles.

Once the intimate is put into play, it does not initially concern what we ordinarily call "sex." (That could be on the order of what we call "emotion" or "thought," but also "gesture," "expression," or "presence"). Quite the opposite. The sexual, before or beyond sex, turns out to be what opens an order distinct from both the order of things and the order of signification. It is an order of *sense*—and the *senses of sense*—where signs are in play but do not make signification; they make pleasure-desire instead. These insignificant signs are gestures, touches, appeals. (At the risk of vulgarity, we should think of the sense of the English *sex appeal* . . .) What is in play is an appeal or call, and we will leave undetermined whether it is a question or order, assignation or request. This appeal can take place between two looks, two intonations, two gestures, with nothing following from it at all. It can even play out from a look (or a hearing, a touch, etc.) directed at something outside the human (animal, material, object) that comes to be sexualized, if not sexed.[12] But in this way it is perhaps also appeal in itself, the sending of a statement without anything being stated. This could be the literal sense of the word *adoration*. (Adoration can remain mute and secret, unknown even to the one adored and in any case far removed from any *passage à l'acte*. The gospels know something about this, convicting of sin anyone who has even "desired a woman in his heart." But rather than embarking on a commentary on Christian guilt, we should think first of the infinitization of desire that is opened up here and the fact that it is perhaps not so far removed from the one opened—in a different way—in Plato's eroticism.)

Whatever form it takes, the opposition between love and desire runs the risk of preserving the Augustinian antagonism between *cupiditas* and *caritas* which has structured a whole field of Christian doctrine. This opposition between nature (the principle of insatiable appetite) and grace (the principle of inexhaustible oblation) proceeds from the infinitization of man and world. By this means it separates itself from the Platonic distinction between love of body and love of soul, since the latter leaves open the way from one register to another as a passage from one order of *forms* (which are by definition not infinite) to another. The movement of this passage is already infinite, but its stages remain defined. Christian infinity is split into the bad infinity of the missing object and the good infinity of the subject of surrection. In any case, it is definitively a matter of this and this alone: no creature is its own essence—but it has its being in a creator who, in the final analysis, has no substance other than relation itself. What flows from this makes *caritas* and *cupiditas* indissociable in the Greek-Christian scheme of things—right at the heart of their intimate dispute. (Perhaps intimacy is created by this very dispute.)

Since then they say that love—Christian or not, philosophical or not, erotic or not—cannot be distinguished without remainder from desire. And, in fact, it is not certain that, under these conditions, they can be opposed at all, even if they also cannot simply be confounded. Love and desire govern and exclude one another, each one representing both the finition and the infinition of the other, each one capable of falling outside the other, while neither can subsist in its essence closed off from the other. There must be love in each gesture of desire and vice versa. But in each case this can tend toward the fading away of one or other of them. Love and desire would thus be the two poles of relation, of its taking place without place, since they themselves stand in a relation without relation. Love gives what is not (according to Lacan), and desire grasps what exceeds it. Somewhere between them is a zone for sharing, whether it is a matter of commerce or collision.

At this point I will again cite a writer, another, very different writer, but nonetheless another of those who know more than we do, as Freud said of the artists. This is Norman Mailer writing about Henry Miller: "yet lust can alter on the instant to love. Indeed, the more intense lust becomes, the more it is out of focus—the line of the ridge between lust and love is exactly where the light is blinding, and the ground remains unknown."[13]

These rival—which is not to say opposing—figures of love and desire are known as fidelity and infatuation [*foudre (celle du coup)*]. The one excludes the other, and in more than one respect. Fidelity does not consist in sustaining a fire whose essence is to consume itself. For this reason there is no transition from one to the other, and the one can destroy the other, just as, if they co-exist, they remain no less heterogeneous. Nevertheless, infatuation and fidelity are also two figures of actual infinity—that is, figures of what is known as eternity: one of consumption, the other of assumption: an eternity present in the instant, an eternity as faith promised beyond all instants. Perhaps there is no eternity without the intimate, divided relation between two. The eternal return is the affirmation of the present beyond all presence. According to this discordant affirmation and according to this properly senseless confidence, infatuation and fidelity, desire and love necessarily appeal to one another—albeit in order to respond, as they always do, beyond all response. This is another way in which desire illuminates itself: as a faith beyond fire, or as a fire that defies all faith.

Therefore, when we do something more than exchange a few signs of appeal, when we *make love* in the proper sense (but what exactly could be the propriety, if not the properness and cleanliness, of such an expression?) it is not that we change the nature of the appeal in some way. (This leads me to add in passing that the idea of "sublimation," as we already know, is decidedly fragile: maybe nothing is ever "sublimated," but everything is susceptible to being sublime . . .). But when we make love, we pose or expose relation *as such*. We pose its "unrelatable" character explicitly. The paradox here is that by making love we expose infinition as such. (We could also say that we pass from the sexuating sexual to the sexed sexual.) What must be produced, at least up to a certain point, is a determination (a "finition") of sexed positions, identities, jouissances. The actors also become those who expose their own infinition. But this is how they experience jouissance: on the threshold of finitude.

Certainly, then, there is no relation in the sense that there is no account to be given and no accountability of excess, not because excess involves a gushing that would go on and on interminably (which would eventually come to the same thing as an oceanic, fusional entropy), but because excess is simply, strictly, and exactly [a matter of] reaching oneself as difference and reaching difference as such, that is, reaching what cannot be examined or instantiated *as such*, unless its "as such" is exposed as what is never *such* (which is what would be required by the idea of an evaluation, measure, or accomplishment of relation). There is in fact no relation *as* relation. Indeed, fucking does not take place *as such*, but always otherwise (what pretends to be fucking *as such* is pornography: it is the only figure of the impossible as impasse). Fucking takes place as reaching or gaining access to its own impossibility, or as its own impossibility as access to whatever element of self-relation is incommensurable with every relation. But we fuck, and by fucking—whatever fucking is—I say again with Celan, our senses are burned. Jouissance is not something we can achieve. It is what achieves itself and consumes itself in that self-achieving, burning its own sense, that is, illuminating it even as it burns it up.

I conclude by suggesting what we might take up on another occasion: we might push further the analysis of a proposition that would be stated like this: *the sexual is the "there is" of relation.*

Coda

A friend, Ariane Chottin, suggests this gloss: the there-is-iad of relation [*l'il-i-a-de du rapport*]. It is true: the double literary monument of our origins, the *Iliad* and the *Odyssey*, together make up a double figure of the sexual, of infatuation and fidelity. The *Odyssey* tells the story of the return, the Periplus that reaches its conclusion in the domestic palace where Penelope weaves the deception of her waiting until the moment when Odysseus comes to take her once again to the bed he made with his own hands. A quest is completed, the bed carved from an olive tree once again serves its original purpose. But the *Iliad*, in contrast, begins in the disorder and fury of the desire of the two kings for their captives, although the war itself came about because of the favor Aphrodite granted when she made it possible for Paris to ravish Helen (to whom, besides, the text is dedicated). When Achilles decides to re-enter combat, his captive is sent back to him, Briseis *of the fair cheeks, fair as golden Aphrodite*. We see the hero for the last time in the poem in bed with her. In the morning, Andromache mourns Hector; dead in combat, he was not even able to reach out his hand to her from his bed, nor to leave her with a word to cherish in her memory. The poem is the jouissance of language and the language of jouissance.

The Birth of Breasts

At that moment, the softness of nudity (the place where legs and breasts begin) touched the infinite.

—**Georges Bataille,** *L'impossible*

Ah, that I were dark and nocturnal! How I would suck at the breasts of light! . . . Oh, it is only you, you dark ones, you nocturnal ones, who create warmth out of that which shines. It is only you who drink milk and refreshment out of the udders of light.

—**Friedrich Nietzsche,** *Thus Spoke Zarathustra*

I

An interminable rise, imperceptible but executed without hesitation, an upheaval, a light, supple tension as far as the extremity of its own termination, which does not stop it but raises it up again and suddenly gathers it in, colors and darkens it, puckers and wrinkles it meticulously so as to resolve its rising form in the perfect, symmetrical replica of a mouth stretched open and relaxed in order to pronounce the word that stands alone—*the breast*—in the naked presence, outside and far beyond all language, of a rise that itself is accomplished in itself, appeased, by a light, mobile lift—an accomplishment always in progress, constantly repeating itself

    not the cold roundness of the sphere of being, nor the insidious curve of the symbol, neither the one nor the other but their parallel, catallel,

23

mutual doubling, the one undoing the other, their reciprocal unconnectedness in a double elevation that is by turns graceful, playful, futile, and rhythmic, the perpetual sending of one to the other, and movement—a movement that owes nothing to muscles and everything to emotion and gravity—that prevents them coming to an end, puts an end to the reign of ends, offering again nothing but weight and its opposite, a summary of elementary physics and the soul of the world, an incessant birth of the world

neither a grand, heroic form nor a lyrical outpouring, nor indeed the circles and angles of the concept, but the need—more pressing than ever, in the end—to turn language back toward what touched it, toward what undid it long before all language, toward what escapes it, the need, desire to turn our hands back toward what at the very beginning hollowed out and filled our palms, running curved palms the length of curves, vases, the clean line of things,

not in an attempt to approach a beginning, to suckle on nostalgia but, on the contrary, in order to learn anew the extent to which it is, itself, the beginning, newer still, in advance, unknown, exposed, of a difference that is not the difference between words and things, nor the difference of one sex from another, nor of nature from technology but rather the difference by which each one of these differences precedes the others indefinitely, each in turn, permitting no rest, disturbing all rest,

(enigma and mystery, calling to the hermaphrodite seer Tiresias, who had the breasts of a woman, with his knowledge, their knowledge, the knowledge of women's breasts resting against the belly—guess what)

obliging us anew, differently, to not let reason seek repose, just as Kant no longer permitted it to think it had found it, flattering itself that it had demonstrated and presented the necessity in itself of the being itself, or God, obliging us therefore to pursue on our own (without God, without Kant either) the elevation of reason toward a termination that brings it to an end with no flaws in argumentation, sure of itself but still laughing at itself, reason that gives no reason, that does not give at all,

that also does not exalt itself in this rising, but descends again, falls again not in the sense of a precipitous fall but in the sense of a calmness that remains without repose, that, despite everything, leaves

a little joy at the heart of aridity.

This is only right. It is as if, in the dereliction of being and the desiccation of becoming, it was necessary to call to mind the most familiar but also most singular signs of exuberance. Or as if, in the face of the avowed humility of man, it was necessary to evoke the quiet pride of woman.

I am entering into this material without offering any demonstration of the importance of my subject. It is not a matter of importance. At least, it has none of the importance of a subject that is important to discuss, that is, an object. I have no wish to consider an object here. I am initiating a movement, I am following an emotion, allowing myself be led by a sense of a slow failing of writing, of thought—that is to say, a failing by writing and thought itself.

"I am following an emotion, I am an emotion" ["*Je suis une émotion*"]. The French language insists on this ambiguity. I head off after an emotion, I am in pursuit of it, I trail after it, in its wake, or, indeed, *I* ("me"?) is an emotion, nothing but that, *ipse* is the incandescent, vanishing point of a fleeting feeling.

I nearly took sick the first time I saw a woman's two breasts completely naked.[1]

No treatise, then, no book of breasts. They exist. I will cite some of them. I've been through as many books as it was possible to go through. There are learned books and grotesque ones, by physicians and voyeurs, courteous gallants and dirty old men. Everything has been said, of course, and it is already too late, or too early.

It's not much different in the breast room of this house. Milk flows out under the closed door and from the keyhole comes a sweet, white smell that makes me feel ill. No sound comes from this room. The silence of the childbed reigns in there. This soft deep silence is something I know well from long ago. Back then I wished that it would go on for ever. Everything has changed terribly, and that's why the breast room inspires nothing but despair in me.[2]

It is, then, a pretext. This subject that is not one is a pretext for talking about other things. What? This is what I still do not know. There is a seduction, an attraction to something that is not quite designated, indeed hardly designateable at all, something adventurous and necessary. Toward a limit of language, but a limit we can touch, a fragile skin. This word, *sein* ["breast"], insinuating, slippery, sensed in a brief rise of the voice and quickly extinguished, abandoned at birth, at its emergence into speech. For it is not like a pure absence. It is not an inaccessible mystery, or it is, like all mysteries, like mystery itself in general and absolutely, the very movement of its own revelation; it is what shows itself and has nothing at all to show except this movement, this presentation and offering of itself. *Pretext*: what is brought forward, what is woven in front, the border of a cloth, lace, braid, the selvedge edge or fringe—what borders and embroiders a thin clothing of self,

> . . . *the swelling of breasts*
> *Beneath a tunic . . .*[3]

The self, in turn, is nothing more than this: carried in front, preceding, presence that goes ahead of all existence and that frustrates sense and desire, the beat of being, the slipping of words out of the dross that conceals them. The self consists precisely in the distance that separates self from itself, and in the return to self that crosses that distance
by recklessly hurling itself across it. One precedes the other without the other knowing—blind chest, closed spots, in front, standing up, opaque flames brandished in front of nothing. Exposed, put out front, displayed, in a shop window, on sale—*prostitutum*—and thus *protectum*, protected by a breastplate or a shield, a pectoral, a chest in front of the chest, covering the depth, covering what rises from the depth of one's breath, the depths of one's heart, *ab imo pectore*, extroverted autism.

Exposed interiority, the *sinus* of the womb raised and opened out into the breast.

So, perhaps a pretext for whatever it is for which all other books and treatises have only been the pretext? The one who writes is always the most prudish and the lewdest of men. But this describes all of us, men and women, without writing, insofar as we appear in front of others in the simple, ordinary rubbing along of being with one another.

> *But the agora is not by any means a small place. In Olynthos, for example, it takes up the space of eight* insulae. *The same is true in Miletus, Priene, all the most theoretical cities. The layout of the city therefore speaks clearly and tells us the importance of these places; yet, clearer still, and what relates them to one another, is that they are anomalies or, rather, events in the space of the city. What makes an event in this case is not really a construction or a monument but a void, an emptiness in the urban fabric. Much more than a notch or a small gap, [it is] an open field right in the bosom of the city that, instead of distancing itself from it, supports, exalts, and resolves it.*[4]

We are so very naked! But what is it that encircles and carries our nudity in front of everyone, in front of all? What is it that always and constantly betrays (as they say) the judgments and most secret traces of our intimate schematism, and that we do not even know? What is it that opens what is closed to us, like this scar between my breasts, under which, I am told, there is a transplanted heart?

Which caress of a silent intruder lays bare the breast, right to the heart?

II

Before calling up an image, the expression *the birth of breasts* does not need to describe or indicate anything else: a reserve, a holding back that contains the possibility, perhaps the necessity, of withdrawal, abstention, a drawing back that makes it possible to throw.

How are we to speak without speaking of any object? How pass from the side of the thing—where it is always ahead of us, always already there, carried in front—how to pass from its side and by its side in order to espouse its movement, the exact mode of its presence and not its representation, the mode of its pre-venance, its going-ahead? How to pass, then, with language to the same thing, how to touch it, hold it, handle it, weigh it, and preserve it with the aim of finally giving it to itself, of leaving it, the thing, quite naked—but with a nudity that is identical to its saying? Saying the naked breast, saying: "the naked breast" [*le sein nu*].

The mouth breaths this light syllable and takes the breast between its lips.

There is nothing else at all at stake in what is known by various names: *literature, poetry, song*, and even *language*, plain and simple, however little we pause to think of it: quite simply the double genitive of an expression such as this: "the saying of the thing." And this is why, behind every book, there is a hidden book, the intimate writing that demands its due, a deep, deaf offering that rises out of nudity and as nudity. The book of the only possibility of books, of their delivery. The book that would save us from all books, from the garish confusion of significations, that would do justice to, but would also come about because of, the exasperation of a point in the depths of the belly, or in the head, the point of juncture and rupture, the cleft of soul/body, the pineal gland in an unbearable state of intimation and intimidation. Me at my most agitated. The double sense of the French word *sein* ["breast" and "womb"] feeds on this twist, which it aggravates and irritates in turn: from the most profound, the heart, kidneys, or womb, to the most superficial, the two seductive buds from which milk can also flow. The double mystery of the rise and exhibition of the thing itself (nothing less, if you think about it, than the proper hysteria of the thing), coming from the depths and the origin, produced by and as surface, as the exorbitant elevation of the human body standing up and there, more extraordinary still, standing before him, available to the senses, the visible precedence of the sharing of soul and body, which, in its greatest depths, is nothing but the surging forth or the initial shudder of language. No mystery, then, but a futile agitation that is touching, laughable.

Yes, it fell from the bud of my breast and I didn't even realize it. Like a manned boat pushing off from the shelter of the rocks without increasing the sea's tremor, without the earth feeling this new adventure, from my Cybelline breast a new poem fell and I didn't even realize it.[5]

How am I to speak in an element that is neither mine nor the world's nor the gods' but that obtains in the single circumscription of a detail, narrow, reserved, discrete, even indistinct and therefore also troubled, vacillating (indiscrete, and therefore insistent, embarrassing and troubling—moving and moved). How?

A detail, almost nothing. Not "the breasts" but their birth, the place where they rise from the chest, as a infinitesimal zone of the body, not exactly delineated, but passing beyond all delineation in order to trace the insensible and make it felt. The universal singular.

It is an imperceptible zone of the body, the beginning of puberty or of a caress. A detached zone, set apart, reserved for a mystery. The moment it is born the whole body sets itself into zones, distributes itself into uncertain territories of multiple revelations. It is born to itself again, in plural births that are re-nascent in turn.

We are attached with infinite delicacy to what I call the birth of the breast, the little fold that, on each side of the cleavage, marks the beginning of the breast's swelling. It is the most sacred place in the beauty of the breast because it is in this absence, in the cleavage of a woman's décolletage, that a man's gaze sees what he imagines. The birth must be perfect so that it can call us to see more.[6]

As far as the bust is concerned, it is the other extreme from the Valaisans. With tightly laced corsets they attempt to give a misleading notion of its firmness; there are other means to give a misleading notion of its coloration. Although I have perceived these objects only from very far off, they are so available for inspection that little remains to be guessed at. These Ladies in this respect seem ill to understand their own interests; for provided the face is agreeable, the observer's imagination would moreover serve them much better than his eyes, and according to the Gascon Philosopher, total hunger is far more acute than hunger that has already been sated, by at least one of the senses.[7]

Then again, it could be that birth is initially in play as the birth of anything at all, not just of the breasts. They themselves, therefore, as a pretext, a text of the body in advance of itself, in this place where "the body" is itself nothing but nascent, a sketch, a rough draft of the soul, of being or of gesture. "Body" is just a rising up, a swelling, the extended, fleeting curve of a distinct passing that pierces the horizon and then disappears.

Finally, to know how to be content with passing—with always having been preceded, with passing, raised-up body stretched out dead immortally at the breast of the earth.

> *The breast is the chest that has been raised to a mysterious state—the moralized breast. Thus, for instance, a deceased person is a person that has been raised to an absolutely mysterious state.*[8]

Death, then, is the assumption of the breast: not the return to the womb but the supreme elevation, the chest raised to the end. The end [*bout*]: it is the result of a driving blow [*coup bouté*], pushed and struck. The nipple [*bouton*] is first of all a bud, a flower not yet in bloom, the first result of the sap's pushing and striking out into the branches. Life pushes death, pushes to death: this is its entire work, its courage. It rises to this immeasurable grandeur; it raises this temple, this dome, this tumulus piled up under the excrescence of an existence. Women carry death emblazoned on the tips of their breasts. Death is a bud: the eternity that resembles time, its zone, its tightly closed enclosure. A small mass of tenacious lumps. Death in the bosom of life—or maybe the other way around—the one generating the other, one thanks to the other. Pinching, calming.

> *. . . love*
> *came back into the beds, the women's*
> *hair began to grow again,*
> *the buttons of their breasts,*
> *long turned to the inside,*
> *came out again, life lines,*
> *heart lines awoke in your hand, climbing along the slope of a hip.*[9]

> *life mixes everything up*
> *and in a nightclub, in front of a*
> *bottle of bad booze, you can*
> *caress its beautiful breasts with a heart full of death.*[10]

But birth itself? Is it itself? Can it merely be, can it be something like "itself"? (Nothing more than a sister to death.)

How then could "something" be the very thing that precedes and prepares the presence of something in general? It would have to be something that, as a result, can have no presence itself. Or could birth itself be something not born, the only thing that is not born but that is simply there, without remainder, without becoming, nothing more than that? It would be being itself, nothing but birth as it is, un-born in some way and so never born and never to be born. But this being cannot be identified with birth in any way. Birth is the figure that is the opposite of being, and thus neither non-being nor becoming. Becoming is continuous passage and alteration. But birth is the coming that has not yet become. It precedes this passage and only opens the way for it. Birth begins, but without being the principle of beginning. It is not the origin; it is not engenderment. It is not punctual but is between the point of origin and the full curve of a presence that has reached the other point, the point of plenitude. It is the capture, the raising up of this curve, this rise; yet, at the same time, this rise itself, in order to rise, to raise itself up, curves space. Thus inflected, it empties it out, sets it at a distance, bends and carves it out even as it cambers and raises it. It opens it and gives it over to the essential—for

> As much as need can effect,
> And breeding, still greater power
> Adheres to your birth
> And the ray of light
> That meets the newborn infant . . . But where is anyone
> So happily born as the Rhine
> From such propitious heights
> And from so holy a womb.[11]

(An almost unbearable impatience takes hold of me when I hear this single word essential, just as it does when I hear the word breasts. It is as if it were the same thing: the same irritation at the unattainable, but also the knowledge of what is essentially unattainable, in order to reach it, the time of decay and extinction, the time of nipping off the heads buds. Birth, essence: this means that woman is hidden in me but doesn't ever flourish there, and that I want her, outside me, before me, with me, with so much impatience at the very tips of my fingers.)

> Sun and July
> Bring onto the sidewalks
> Flocks of breasts.[12]

Brust in German, *breast* in English also have the tonality of upheaval, blossoming, budding. It is always a matter of a rising, an expansion of what we have every right to call a proffering: a declaration of sense. The breasts are sense raised up, elevated, promising, offering—a sublimity.

III

Space curved, heaved up, detached from the straight lines of a map, space that is not simply of the order of intersection and position, and also not of the order of terminated, determinate contours, the space of movement though not displacement, the slipping of its own drift, the infinitesimal flux of its own difference, space surging up out of space itself—this is the space we call time. This point does not stay pinned down, limited to its own nature as a dimensionless point, nor is it just repeated to infinity according to some indifferent punctuality. Rather, it opens to this very nature—to its own negativity, Hegel says—and opens it as the difference of an event: to not simply be right at and, as a result, to always no longer be there, and to always not yet be there. Elsewhere. To be in place elsewhere.

> She was so young! Younger than she seemed with her clothes on. Yes, and the painters and sculptors had deceived him: nothing had prepared him for the fact that her breasts, only beginning to grow, would have this elongated, spindly shape, with their too long pink tips. They reminded him of the first growth of certain prairie flowers that, when they begin to grow, push up through the soil a thin, mauve stem with a white base.[13]

Space and time are the two names for birth, the double name that is needed in order for it to come, the bending, raising of an event, neither point nor present (neither space nor time) but presentation (fading away).

Space is no longer just spread out and riddled with marks, time is no longer just successive and irreversible, but the one is opened by the other and not only opened but opening: opening the place, and the taking place of place.

> She spoke, then from her breasts unloosened the pierced and embroidered strap on which all sorts of allurements are brightly emblazoned;
> there upon it is affection, upon it desire and seductive
> dalliance which robs even a sensible person of wisdom.
> This [Aphrodite] put in [Hera's] hands and spoke these words, calling upon her:
> "There, now, here is a strap which you put into your bosom,
> well-embroidered, on which all things are emblazoned."[14]

The space-time of the birth of breasts: taking place as such, perceivable in its pure state, grasped in its raising up, and thus what is left of the very young girl throughout the life of a woman, there at the birth of her breasts, there at the opening of her blouse.

What remains for all her life: life.

What remains of life for life: birth itself, very gentle and very dangerous birth. The chest that rises and that releases air, that draws air to it, and hands and lips, eyes, gestures, and thought.

IV

To open is not only to break apart and separate. It is also, and in the same movement, a matter of forming the opening, disposing it in itself, the curvature and allure by which its use will be defined; it is the rhythm and intensity of a coming, of an abandon that lets being come to be; it is its outpouring, its disgorging.

The opening is the imprint of the outside, of its infinity. But it is not an immobile seal embedded in wax that then hardens and sets; rather than an imprint [empreinte] it is just a span [empan], the time of the beat that hollows out and heaves up a wave, a gulf, a gorge, a sinus. The wave is the opening encounter—not operative but inoperative—between two closed immensities, the one of water and the other of air, two immobilities, two immanences, two immaturities curved and rolled against each other.

I tried to pull her body toward me. I quickly felt her breasts, very volu-minous and very beautiful, as they pressed against me. Némie's breasts touched me, came into contact with my torso; I remember finding that sensation completely incredible.[15]

and then
born of the wind or the pull of the moon—gravitation, curvature of space in the vicinity of great masses—or both at once, a rising up, an ascent, the gathering of the swell, the shudder of a wave—its difference—from the trough to the crest, the oscillation and suspended balance, sustained, propagated, transmitted from place to place; mobile but in turn immobile in the logical repetition of the always altered same, the immature imma-nence, almost immaterial, set outside itself and taking form, pushed from place to place like the same place taken up again and exchanged, never localized, always pushing back the horizon and raising it up from its hori-zontality at every moment, making it crenellated, notched, breached, dispersed—

A breast hardly expressed anything. It is the face one consults to know the kind of character one is dealing with. The women, moreover, among themselves look each other in the eye, but they do not look at each other's bodies. . . .

I remember having been struck and disillusioned many a time . . .
by the fact that a woman's breasts, when I happened to see them uncov-
ered, were only beautiful, while the face was so wrought by intelligence,
by a soul so odd and so exceptional, that I had been persuaded somehow
that the breasts too would be exceptional and original. But a breast is
not a face.[16]

—elevation, raised up, not the vertical, not the right angle or the ortho-
normal mark, but rather the curve that escapes at every point of its inflec-
tion, that drifts away on a tangent. It touches in order to move away,
touches as it moves away furtively, fleetingly, a system of flight and contact, passing to the limit, like an *über*-generalized law of being that makes
it tremble, like its most ancient law.

Raise her breast to me
Nice, white, shining, broad, half open and full.
Inside, a thousand flooding veins
Flow full with red blood.
Then, when you see it naked, you discover
Muscles and nerves beneath the skin
Swollen on top, two new apples,
As if we were looking at two green apples
On an orange tree, which have nothing at all to do
But, at the right time, turn red to their tips.[17]

The most general law (birth and death, soul and body, raising up and
setting down, between the two a smooth and syncopated continuity—the
breast, breasts: the discrete presentation of the continuity of the thing, its
intimacy) is no longer a law, it is no longer distinguished as the law of a
pure matter of fact. Rightly so: it is no longer distinguished. It is not abolished. It is still the law, but the law that escapes itself, carried off in the
very simple disposition of being—to be born, to be picked up, to be carried off. Many cultures, maybe the majority, seem to prefer high breasts,
more often than not higher than they naturally are. Elevation gets elevated, and the desire is to restore its youth, the moment of its surging
forth. But the breast lowers gently toward a mouth or toward a hand,
toward the earth. It obeys its weight; it weighs lightly. It eventually col-
lapses, unable to sustain itself any more, but its abandon is always moving:
it continues to be born.

Men who love men also love their breasts, their vestigial tips. Women
who love women touch breast to breast just as men and women sometimes touch penis to breasts, a fable of milk-sperm, the communication
of idioms.

Is this a dream? No: the clear
Rubies of raised breasts still kiss the quiet
Air,
And I drink in sighs.[18]

And what is that flutter like a torn leaf, quivering
Still in the islands of my naked breast?[19]

From time to time—and it is time itself, its distinct sameness—another sort of wave comes to a standstill on the surface, and it is an island, the result of another rising, another folding of the depths. A place apart, an autonomous place, a place closed over on a strangeness, the place of an unknown tribe, fierce or weak, a place for the shipwrecked, a place for the absence of humans or for a new beginning. Also from time to time an island disappears under the sea, reclaimed by another movement of the depths, by another wave that begins far down in the magma on which the slow, heavy tectonic plates float. The drift of continents, the unimaginable reconfiguration of the world, ancient and new worlds, over millions and millions of years. There time, in its turn, becomes space once again.

We can feel at every moment the pounding of the waves, and how disconcerting it is to be there, isolated on that small island.

> *The tip of the breast is also in an isolated position in relation to its background, and by virtue of this fact it is in a position of exclusion regarding the deep relation the infant has with the mother . . . Think of those islands you see on nautical maps. Nothing on the island is represented, only the perimeter. Well, the same goes for objects of desire in all their generality.*[20]

V

The wave or the island is the very birth of sense:

> *the wave taken in itself can be thought of as breaking apart into air and water (this is the necessary relation between the existence of wind and the existence of water; there is no wave if one of the two elements is missing). Moreover, the breeze taken in itself generally blows in a straight line and does not undulate; as for the water in itself, it tends toward immobility. In short, the form of the wave is analogous neither to the "form" of the wind nor the "form" of the water ("arbitrary" relation). Moreover, it is an illusion to think that one wave can exist in isolation; we must consider the whole ensemble. That is the effect—*

unique and multiple at once—of the breeze passing over the surface of the whole lake. Not only does each wave break into water and wind, but even without breaking it apart, the wave can be analyzed from two points of view. On the one hand, it represents the effects of the wind on this limited area of the surface; on the other, it exists only through the other waves' "articulating" the amorphous mass of water across its whole surface. In the same way, says Saussure, language is articulated in signs by the meeting of thought/sound. Each sign can be seen as the particular meeting of this thought and this sound, but in fact this thought and this sound do not pre-exist their meeting. In a single movement this melting involves the general flux of thought and the general flux of sounds. It exists only through other signs. More precisely, a given sign exists only thanks to what allows other signs to exist.[21]

This sign is neither a signal nor a symbol of something else: neither thought nor sense come before it, nor do they survive it. It is not there for the sake of something else, it is the *there*, the taking place of a differing and deferring of existence. (*Signum*, which has the same origin as *sectio* or *segmen* is no doubt originally a mark that is incised, the opening of a distance, the birth of significance, signature and *seing*.[22] The *there* that opens *elsewhere*, that opens even here a possible elsewhere.

The seing *does not suffer to be illegible in this respect. If, at least, reading means (to say) to decipher a sense or to refer to something. But this illegibility that takes form by falling (from my hand, for example), that scrambles and broaches signification, is that without which there would not be any text. A text "exists," resists, consists, represses, lets itself be read or written only if it is worked (over) by the illegibility of a proper name. I have not—not yet—said that the proper name exists, or that it becomes illegible when it falls (to the tomb) in the signature. The proper name resounds, losing itself at once, only in the instant of its debris, when it is broken, scrambled, jammed, while touching, tampering with the* seing.[23]

The point of the breast will always be promised to the impossible.[24]

There is where we find the meeting of masses, or flux, masses as flux, but if these fluxes are not distinct before they meet, then the meeting is also the division of a single flux, which is also not distinguished as "flux" or as "mass": indistinction itself, or water in water. The single articulated flux—"language," thought/sound, soul/body, intimacy/extimacy—itself becomes distinct only by being distinguished *from self in itself*. It is this unity in two only in this instantaneous upheaval, already uncoupled in/

from itself, unfolded—the fold of two *seings* at the same time, and more than two, very ancient many-breasted goddesses, or indeed modern-day mutants multiplying their breasts: the imagination fails on the edge of food or pleasure, at the approach of the milk of jouissance.

She alone rises, bare-breasted, in the sense that she consumes.[25]

The fold, the bosom [*gorge*] that is sense, gathers itself into a unity that is suddenly heaved up, presented, ready to pour itself into a mouth or a hand—but at the same time it slips away just like that, spurting out of itself. The very thing that would like to be represented as the happiness of the word, the grace of sense, the favor of expression, is also the pinch and irritation of separation, the susceptibility that makes it stand up, erect, and makes it recede right there, closed, hard, intensifying the irritation of insignificance, the waiting, and the anxiety of a satisfaction that it grants and refuses at the same time.

The breast retains what it exposes: its own gift. The breast is the gift. It is the gift of self. It is the "self" of the gift, the ipseity of the gift, which is not the ipseity of any subject but is its own subject, up to the point where it is not a subject but, precisely, a breast, breasts, the breasts of women and the breasts that are still to be found on the chests of men.

Sense immediately outside itself—which is what defines it.

Thought: in this ejaculation, this erection or election that binds the movement of the chasm, the nothing, [there is] no sense, no presence. Thought as impatience and annoyance, as exasperation at not being the representation or signification of anything at all but rather the surging forth of self; it is what surges out of itself, and is nothing but surging.

"There now, look," he went on, pointing to Albertine and Andrée who were waltzing slowly, tightly clasped together, "I've left my glasses behind and I can't see very well, but they are certainly keenly roused. It's not sufficiently known that women derive most excitement through their breasts. And theirs, as you see, are touching completely."[26]

Not the tranquility of a picture hung in me like an idea but, rather, what rises up and threatens to rip open the canvas, or what rises behind it, a touch, a stain, a paste and the spatula that applies it.

As a result, nothing survives of an already given "self"—but the self that consists in surviving: not remaining the same that it is not and will never have been. The self surges forth, rises up and is thereby outside itself but, all the while, and identically, it is turned back on itself. The wave is not a modification of water or air. The island is not a modification of earth or fire, air or water. It is not a matter of there being elements and then their modifications. Modification is elementary.

Thought is modification: the rise of a mode, that is to say a measure, cadence, rhythm, scansion, form, contour, motif, figure, way, turn, manner. It is what is modalized in and of itself, measured and cut up, modified without ever having been something modifiable; indeed, the modifiable is all that substance shows without itself.

It is what . . .—a leap within itself where there was no being for itself. A leap out of itself in itself, and what leaps also passes over itself, misses or evades or empties itself at the same time. Neither aseity nor perseity; ipseity, perhaps.

But there is no reflexive in *ipse*, no itself. *Ipse* consists of *is* (this here) with *pse* ("intensifying particle"). This here, particularly intensified. It*self*, in this way accentuated, erected, set upright, distinguished, separated. Flexion without reflection. Pre-reflexive, unreflected, what surges forth. It there, here, on the right or left, nowhere else, not between the two but the one or the other and therefore with the other on one side or the other of an interval, a valley, a fold of co-existence.

It surged forth exactly where it finds itself, and what does it find?

I am the breast.[27]

It, reinforced. It, insistent. At the same time desisting, withheld, collapsed, weighing toward the ground, but always softly raising the affirmation of softness itself: I am here, I am nothing but the being of this "here," its possibility, its availability.

Neither activity nor passivity: availability.

His fingers pinched her nipple, once, and slid quickly out again.[28]

(Born not once but twice: at the tip its color deepens and its texture puckers, point or button, the peak of the breast as though detached from it, hard, tight, grainy, wrinkled, or maybe even wide, lost in its own areola—something that softly tears apart, comforts and excites, that grips beauty, something that excites the heartrending desire for beauty. But it still remains to be seen whether it is beauty that rends our hearts or rather the desire for it, or if they are the same thing and if beauty is itself the desire for beauty, always more and less than itself, always outside itself, strange and inconsequential.)

VI

. . . Thought: there is always talk (a dream?) of an unthinkable object, of the unthinkable thing in the depths of the object, in the depths of the subject, in the depths of the depths. Always weighing the imponderable. Thought weighs [*la pensée pèse*]; this is what the word means. It weighs the weight of intensification and the upheaval of the imponderable thing. Like pumice stone, porous, rounded, floating in the waters around volcanic islands—until the sea seems sprinkled with a mineral, dancing Milky Way. Lean overboard, slip a hand into the water and take one of these lightened, un-stoned pebbles. You can feel it in your hand, quiet, light, inert and mobile.

An infinite lightness, nothing but being pure and simple, insignificant, evanescent, on the edge of vanishing, so similar to nothingness—but just *similar*, not identical but, rather, equal, paired and matched, nothingness we can touch. Nothing but that, suddenly raised up, heaved up *as such*.

And in the water, the almond-white swimmers,
The silvery water glazes the upturned nipple . . .[29]

Imagine: being as being. Virtually unimaginable. Unrepresentable. The condition of all presentation, all coming, all rising up. It must be imagined to be unimaginable. Not an image, the scheme of an image, an imperceptible image, an art hidden in the depths of nature, possessing an element of surprise that can never be appropriated, the turn of hand for turning an image, for giving a turn to what remains blind and empty in the depths, waiting to be raised—awaiting the *similar*, being's match.

That which is not thinkable but which thinks: suddenly weighing on itself, letting its weight be felt, bending under its own singular allure, folding thanks to its own folds—itself, what is called *being*, being nothing but its own fold. Being pure and simple—absolute being—is nothing unless it is at least in itself: being implicated in itself, it needs to be folded back, and this folding back raises and unfolds it, deploys and bends it, explains and opens it toward its own exposed enigma.

The Sphinx has breasts; it exposes itself as enigma:

the sphinx without question the round breast confused in front and so without answer and without word is this a grain of coffee a φ a sex a θ she prowls about like what cannot quite be recalled, the closest, the thought-man remember that there is something.[30]

Goddess of death, the Sphinx, offering this generous death that is so difficult to accept because it is the taking away of all objects—but an infinite thing. Impossible to accept, but sweet nonetheless.

Always remember to think an unthinkable object or subject; force yourself to speak of something unnameable. Always be in touch with what removes itself from contact. Always want to put some supplementary line or plane between the arc and its tangent, some supernumerary point with its halo, its little areola, its circular area softly indicating the imminence of the riddle.

An unthinkable object: not exactly an object, but a thing; the thing itself and not even the thing but the heart of the thing. *Why* there is something. Through which there is upheaval, folding, complication and offering of being.

Life-giving forces bathed her as if they had suddenly found in her breast, consecrated to death, the vainly sought meaning of the word "life-giving."[31]

Why: for the *what* of the thing itself. For its presence and contingence, for nothing. The breast for nothing, for its infinite birth.

Not an object, and certainly not what is known as a "partial object." All objects are partial, but desire has no object. Desire is precisely to be without object—exactly like being; desire is the birth to self of being, the generative fold. Desire is raised to the point of infinite ending, to the point of an area filled and darkened with a very strange, very singular, and very appropriate abolition of self.

The thought of the "partial object" is an impoverished thought, a thought of lack. (Yes, of course we are lacking: we lack the knowledge that there is nothing lacking, but if we knew that, if we were full of that knowledge, we would not have the unsettling thought of desire, birth and death: being would be emotionless.)

The thought of the partial object assumes that there is a piece that comes in the place of what has been lost or is inaccessible; it is an impoverished thinking that turns the breast into a paradigm of partial objects and thus demonstrates that it is capable of conceiving only a breast that is itself partial, cut off, separated from its birth, from the place where it rises, from its chest, torso, shoulder and arm, neck, throat and belly, an abstract breast, a fetish that is equivalent to any number of other fetishes that are just as castrated, penis, turd, or little stuffed animal, partial, transitional objects—they say—objects in transition, yes, commodities circulating in order—they say—to fill up a threatening void.

(Yes, there is a threat, there is fear of the abyss that opens up at the end of the blind alley of life. And it is no use preaching that we just have to put up with it. We cannot just put up with it. But whoever does not feel this emotion cannot even feel that he feels nothing.)

(Touching with the tips of the fingers, as though to close the eyes.)

I love those paintings that make me want to pass my hand across the breast or the back of the figure, if the painting is of a woman.[32]

Thus for them, bit by bit, each and every being becomes just such a partial object; the void and the absence of sense open up everywhere. They confuse the breast with the mammary—after all, mammaries are also part of the body of female animals, rising softly from the belly, sometimes several of them, some of them heavy and pendulous, some of them hardly peeping out at all, and sometimes simply folds of skin around imperceptible sources of milk—and they even confuse it with the nipple, the end for sucking, or with the protuberance, the big fat, rolly breast, vaguely infantile and heavily libidinous.

The martyrdom of Saint Agatha and her holy companions, all of whom were subjected to the same torment, is the savagery of removing the breasts, making them into a double object that is now nothing more than a ball cut in two, and that no longer has anything of the infinitely slow curve of a rise and fall—breasts brutally, atrociously laid on a plate.

> three Polish women . . . who had been subjected to "medical experiments" in the German concentration camp of Ravensbrück. One of them had been unnecessarily operated on against her will. The other had received an injection in the breast, which afterward turned hard and black and had to be amputated.[33]

The *Saint Agatha* by Francesco Guarino does not show her breasts. She presses to her chest a bloodied cloth, which she holds as she would hold her breast, using a gesture that is always repeated in painting and sculpture: the woman covering her breasts with her hands, showing them even as she hides them, supporting them, protecting them, offering them, as if the whole body participated in the turn and fold of the breast. She looks at me in a way that bothers me: she invites me to know that her breasts are there, right against the bloody torso, right against the trace of blood, inviolable and unalterable—some touches of red that are the only color in the painting, the painting itself. With the tips of her fingers buried in the cloth, she touches and invites us to touch the birth of her breasts that the torment was powerless to suppress (and that no wound, no cancer can suppress): rather, it has revealed it.

The scar is still the breast. This is not an object that an executioner would show his pals for a laugh and then throw in the fire or to the pigs. It is right at the body of Agatha—Agathe, "the good," "the excellent"—it belongs to that body in a way that makes it inalienable, unsacrificeable, it is its holiness, its secret, and the top of this chest and this naked shoulder say nothing less than all other bare-breastedness. Nothing less, for there is nothing more to state than the statement itself, nothing else to promise than the promise, the disruption of an infinite good.

Lisa thinks about Zurbaràn's young martyrs: the Sicilian girl who car-
ries her breasts on a plate like fresh loaves of bread . . . her hand wrinkles
while holding the dish of earth, almost as if she were afraid of seeing it
slip out, the banquet of her flesh of which Quinziano partook: those two
breasts, balanced between lust and death, on a plate held with two
hands above the infinite abyss of excision. Those two breasts, perfect and
perfectly cut—so perfect that they seem just made, puffed up in a warm
oven and ready for the table—by now are no more than two monuments
to solitude, its two smallest monuments.[34]

This very thing has become so difficult for us to conceive, to receive: that an inexhaustible promise is still a promise (love, death, life) and that in order to make it inexhaustible it is not exactly necessary to exhaust it. (It is not necessary to keep it; it must remain promised.) We have tasted voluptuousness—oh! this terrible word that went from heavy classicism to gluttonous romanticism—that is to say, the taste of pleasure, and we can no longer perceive how pleasure is not tasted but is carried beyond taste along a perfect curve. Always a point, negativity heaved up, circled with a halo of sainthood.

The negativity of breasts is not in their fantastical detachment but in this rise of the body in which is gathered and insistently exposed all the various rises of the body—thighs, belly, shoulders, lips, mound of Venus. This is negativity that is not a moment but an end: elevation for itself, for nothing, for the pleasure of it, for the pleasure that is nothing but the delicate science of vanishing into birth itself, of dissipation in one's own enumeration. All pleasure is a perfume, the birth of breasts is a perfume.

Taste and distaste, good taste and bad taste, the subject and the object: between the two, the sublime, grotesque torment of the pressing desire to experience jouissance, and indeed to experience it, in this same spirit.

There is a panting (a suckling?), a pestering that replaces the sense of the infinite—but the infinite here, now, fleeting.

this filthy, stinking ape, with her false breasts.[35]

The morality of taste bores us as much as the other sort. And for the same reason, which has nothing to do with the beautiful or the good, from which nothing can release us, but rather with the gesture and tone of the moral lesson that brandishes them under our noses like objects, even though the beautiful and the good, like the true and the one and— eventually—like being, are precisely the beyond, beyond-object, the infu- riating beyond.

We have to completely reinvent desire and pleasure. All, almost nothing: how it has no object. (To reinvent what we know perfectly well, knowledge we sucked with the breast.)

> *The bride hath awakened. Lo! She feels her shaking*
> *Heart better all her waking!*
> *Her breasts are with fear's coldness inward clutched*
> *And more felt on her grown,*
> *That will be hands other than hers be touched*
> *And will find lips sucking their budded crown.*[36]

VII

No, no object, no object at all. Thought is not of an object or desire or pleasure. As Kant says, what is concerned with objects is cognition. But thought is of something else (it is of another country, as they say). *It is of the thing itself.* Thought is of this *sameness* of the thing by which the thing comes to arise, detached from itself and staggered, carried ahead of itself. Thought is the rising of the thing.

And therefore of the heart of things. The heart of things is not an object. It is not a function of cognition, it is a space of birth.

Birth is the opening of a space. It invents the spacing that it itself is, the spacing by which a new place takes place. The birth of breasts spaces them from one another: between them they hold their secret, their gorge, their separation, their gathering.

Always speak of it like this: not of an object but of the heart of things—and insofar as we have reached the heart of things. Not as such, but insofar as it is: only in this way can it be "such." There it is—transported. It is this elsewhere place in which and as which existence happens as the same thing as the thing, existence happens in the *same way as the thing.*

"I am the breast"—*Ich bin die Brust* (*Brust* is feminine, and this *Ich* is irresistibly masculine, coming from the pen of Freud, who was, of course, attuned to all this.)

I am this very thing, this, which is there outside me—and which it is impossible for me to be.

> *. . . his cherub's hand*
> *cossets covering the breast index finger tickling the nipple touch touches*
> *   curling curl . . .*[37]

But this very thing is first of all, by itself, the thing that comes out, that shows itself, that is born in the fold and rise. I am this protrusion, this elevation and exposition. This does not mean that "I" am "there": there is not first a "me," then its position in space-time, but rather I am this "there," I am *the* "there" as such, this opening, distinction, elevation, yearning, and this hollowing out. It is not an alienation or alteration of "me," for it does not survive "me" like an accident or a secondary modification of its primary constitution. Modification is primary. This is what birth is: the coming of a "me" by the "me" of a coming. A "self" that rises somewhere, because "somewhere" is opened or offered as a "self." To be opened and offered to oneself, and therefore to you.

What is a self? It is what relates to itself, returns to itself, comes to itself again, proves itself, feels deeply, is affected. It is therefore what does not remain in itself, or rather what is modulated deep inside like an outside for itself, like an immanent exteriority where identity, function, finality are lost, but lost before ever having been there and in order to be there, in order to return and reach themselves as this loss, this extension and distension, this unmooring, this unrolling of the line and the chart where a volume has just been rolled up, and this dis-connection from territory according to which a world is possible:

> only humans have lips, in other words, the outward curling of the interior mucous membranes; only human females have breasts, in other words, deterritorialized mammary glands: the extended nursing period advantageous for language learning is accompanied by a complementary reterritorialization of the lips on the breast, and the breast on the lips.[38]

(A world is possible? But on condition that it is not a traffic territorialized in the master places of the market, which starves half the world and makes it work for nothing, where children's breasts and buttocks are sold to scum. But a world is always a protest against the unworld [*l'immonde*]. A world is a world-will, an absolutely unheard of cosmological demand. Liberty leading the people, her breasts bare, and Gavroche beside her brandishing his pistols. It's Voltaire's fault, and Rousseau's.)

> Ah, dear lover! Wherever you are, whatever you are doing at the moment I write this letter, at the moment your portrait is receiving all that your idolatrous Lover addresses to your person, do you not feel your charming face being bathed with the tears of love and sorrow? Do you not feel your eyes, your cheeks, your lips, your breast, pressed, crushed, overwhelmed with my ardent kisses? Do you not feel your whole being inflamed with the fire of my burning lips?[39]

It is always, then, a question of speaking, not of an object—
(One can no longer talk about an object, all objects, the speech-object, and this is even as the book hidden behind all books shows through, the enlightened book [*le livre délivré-vivant*], satori.)

—and not of some unnameable or unthinkable. Not an unnameable but what makes all names spurt out, and not an unthinkable because there is no such thing, if being and thinking are the same thing. The "unthinkable" is the reserve in being of a thought that is always higher, always one fold and one *sinus* more.

Thinking is nothing but the identical emerging from itself, by which it becomes what it is, emerges from its indifference and presents itself as its other. There is no need to add "I think" to "I am" because "I am" already thinks that it is, and without this thought it would not be. It is not that "only what thinks is," but rather this fact: that it thinks, and that it thinks it, and that it thinks itself in this way, whatever it can think. "I am the breast," thinks the rising up of being, the respiration needed to say it, to say oneself in a breath outside the self. The breast, each time one's own. [*Le sein, chaque fois sien.*]

"I am" forms the breast of thought. It does not say which one I am but, in thinking, this is also thought: that it is neither said nor known which one it is, but, whatever it is, it thinks that it is. It thinks (itself) along with all things that are because it would not be if it could not, by saying "I am," indicate simultaneously the co-propriety of being that it shares with all things. If it were alone, it would not say that it was. It would not say it even for itself. If it says it, it says that others apart from itself could say it or expose it. It thinks the coexistence of these things—strange labor, weight of the chest that rises up in order to try to reach the height.

> My soul can manage . . . Go! adorn some ruin!
> Here it can lose its troubles on my shadow,
> On my breast, at night, gnaw at the charming rocks,
> It sucks the milk of reverie there for hours . . .
> I only sacrificed my naked shoulders
> To light; and on my chest still honey-smooth,
> Whose tender birth rounded out the sky,
> The shape of the world was just coming to rest.[40]

The being of things that are is not itself a thing, but it is the there of the thing. For the being of the *there* is *over there*, from a distance, through there (*illic, illac*), at an indeterminate distance, there in front, separated from *here*; in fact, *here* only leads toward it, is only lifted up and carried along. This is what being *is*. There is nothing to be said about it except this: there—over there. It is the *there* of the taking place of the thing, its coming, its birth, what makes it so that it is not nowhere but on the contrary here where the *no* of nowhere, quite naked, rises and curves and inclines toward being—or, rather, there where the no rises, itself naked, extended being.

Extended: exposed and stretched by each other. Raised, set upright. Separated, erected. Awakened, excited. Dilated, stretched. Moved, swung. Fallen away, gathered in again.

> *Between the arms in man (in other animals between the forelegs) is what is known as the breast. In man the breast is broad, and reasonably so, for the arms are placed at the side and so do not in any way prevent this part from being wide. In the quadrupeds, however, it is narrow because as they walk about and change their position the limbs have to be extended forwards. And on this account, in quadrupeds, the mammae are not on the breast. In man, on the other hand, as the space here is wide, and the parts around the heart need some covering, the breast is fleshy in substance and the mammae are placed on it and are distinct. In the male they are themselves fleshy for the reason just given. In the female, Nature employs them for an additional function (a regular practice of hers, as I maintain), by storing away in them nourishment for the offspring. There are two mammae because the body has two parts, the right and the left. In the case of women they are firmer, but separated, which is accounted for by the ribs being joined together at this place and also so that the nature of the mammae should not be at all burdensome.* [41]

VIII

Because painting paints this persistence of things out in front of themselves, that is, the persistence that pushes them to the surface and sets them—alongside us—on the fragile threshold of their appearing and fading away, the threshold where we disappear with them behind the veil and into the varnish of appearance itself, obscure to itself but shedding light ahead through the thickness of its glaze, for this reason, in order to testify to this secret desire, it—painting—has always included women's bosoms among its preferred subjects:

> *Fresh from the bosom of her mother wave,*
> *Weed of the sea yet mantling her, her flanks*
> *With salt foam yet a-ripple, ye behold*
> *Kypris the all-desired, in what guise*
> *Apelles drew her, beauty penetrant,*
> *No picture, nay, a being warm, alive.*
> *See, how the subtle fingers wring her hair,*

While from her eyes in light soft-streaming flows
A yearning peaceful-poignant: lo, the breast
Swells like a fruit in summer, sign of full
Ripeness at hand.[42]

Painting shows breasts and in showing them shows itself: the spot of color where the contour is completed and where every interpretation—along with every genealogy—is lost as though in an inverted navel. But painting still shows the showing of breasts, the woman presenting her throat and chest, and it strips away any pretext to do with mythology or nursing in order to show that the model is simply showing her breasts at the request of the painter—Raphael, Tintoretto, Corot, Manet, Gauguin—in the service of no title other than *Woman with Bare Breasts*—but that itself is a pretext, the greatest dissimulation, because this title is itself like a halo of glory around their art, the exposition of the essential relief and the unmoving image of the graceful movement of the paintbrush.

Adding a finer touch, brown or carmine, of a point whose sightlessness doubles the model's eye, which is turned toward the ones who are staring at her and who, perhaps believing they are going to feast their eyes, find themselves transfixed by this extremity—

by a precious stone, ruby, sardonyx, agathe, onyx or cornelian, the concretion and contraction of what moved and shone vaguely beneath the dross.

Gem.

Here he did not move at all, with the look of the sun, the breast,
And in rain and dew he did not speak to her in friendship;
I wondered about this and foolishly said: O Mother
Earth, do you, as a widow, always lose time?

. . .

But perhaps you are warmed one day by the ray of heaven,
Its breath gently waking you out of a restless sleep;
So that, like a seed, you break open the old shell,
Break free and the light greets the unleashed world
The whole assembled force flares up in exuberant Spring,
Roses glow and wine sparkles in the barren North.[43]

My heart beats, beats . . . My breast burns, drags me onwards . . .
Oh how it swells, fills out and stretches, hard,
This softest witness, imprisoned in my webs of azure . . .

In me, hard—but so soft against the infinite mouth! [44]

Being—*das Sein* in German (Jean Luc Godard, in *JLG/JLG*, shows Heidegger's *Being and Time* [*Sein und Zeit*] and then a breast [*sein*]). You have to laugh. What can you say? The ek-sistence of the breast, being in the world. Or even *Sein* differentiating itself from *Wesen*. This last means being as sojourn, a stop, a mode of arriving and remaining, staying [*demeurer*]. It is being as staying (essence). There is a part of the conjugation of *sein* that maintains the connection with this root, but it is also attached to another one—*bheu*—that suggests growth and becoming, coming to presence. It is a matter of remaining or presenting oneself, of being as an imposing presence or as mere presence; we must choose.

> *Tania doesn't want me to forget those growing buds she sports . . . she hasn't had them for very long, and she's proud as a pigeon about them. I've got to play with them; I must bite them, give the nipples a chew now and then or she'd feel that I didn't appreciate her. That's the one thing that Tania will sometimes stop fucking for . . . to have those teats of hers played with.*[45]

It is a matter of the heart of things, or the breast of them. The breast more than the heart and sooner than the heart. The heart is merely fixed, punctual. Immobile as such, it has the punctuality of a beat. The heart is always impassible, an unbendable bending point. But the breast envelops and develops the heartbeat. It buries and frees it. The heart is stable, the breast unstable, moving, moved.

In Kantian language, the heart is the mathematical principle and the breast the dynamic principle. The first concerns only the *compositio*, the second the *connexio*. The one engages relation and the order of ends while the other engages only assembly and the order of law. It is a matter of nothing less than the two meanings of *cum*: "with" and "together." The juxtaposed and the entwined.

> *The first room was full of women, and the eye alighted at once on an array of bare breasts, emerging from billows of brilliant drapery. . . . Some fifteen couples were dancing; the men solemn, the girls with a smile fixed on their lips. Like their mothers they showed a good deal of skin, and the bodices of one or two were secured by only a narrow ribbon over the shoulders; now and then one might glimpse a dark stain under the arms. . . . Her face was full of life, alight with happiness. Her warm white skin, the skin that goes with auburn hair, seemed to sparkle. . . . she stayed standing there before him, her bare, heaving bosom offered to the young man's gaze.*[46]

Still, the distinction is not set in stone. There is no side by side without exchange, just as there is no intermingling without distance. What there is not, ever, in any way, is pure exteriority, just as there is no pure interiority. From the moment they are set in opposition neither means anything: each is the pure and simple abolition of sense, since they both forbid any sort of return. For there is no sense without return—to the same or the other, which amounts to the same (that is, the other), provided that there is return. What is needed is a call, recall, restitution, repercussion, resonance, return, reprise, reflection, reproduction, so that there can be coming, and coming is needed for there to be a stay [*séjour*]. *Sein und Wesen, Sein des Wesens und Wesen des Seins* are a match. *Und*: "and"—there must be *and*, conjunction, coordination, an ordering of separation and closeness, of the with that goes from the one to the other and that goes with the one and the other.

How is one to stay, if one has not come to stay? How to come, if not to stay? But this is too simple. Staying is not the end of coming. It still must come to itself in itself, without which the stay [*séjour*] itself is adjourned [*ajourné*], has not put itself in order. And it is also necessary to stay in the coming, to remain in passing and not to pass it by at the risk of negating it.

Sometimes we are exactly between the two, or beside them. We neither come nor stay. We pass on as quickly as possible, or we remain grudgingly, or both at once: more present, more presence. The point of the instant no longer spreads into an areola. At this moment in our time we have the feeling that there is a world there. But perhaps this feeling is neither very new nor any more acute than at other times. Presence is always what is lacking and what, therefore, is always arriving. But today the world is represented as always on its way out. In any case, it is true that the world is what represents being. In order to transform the world we have to change its representation. We must exchange the representation of a presence in flight for a representation of an imminent presence, a coming that we will be able to reign in without stopping.—"We must": it is not a duty but an imploring. There is unhappiness and what is needed is tenderness, not pity.

> *. . . delicacy of spirit frightens me (almost),*
> *good little girl (what's white, etc.:*
> *breasts, from navel to knees, and calves).*[47]

IX

The world is the presentation of the real (of the thing). The thing is presented "as such," "in reality." Simply posing it is nothing; it must be posed again "as such." Like itself, ready to go. [*Pareille à elle même, apare-illée.*] This "as such" is its birth. Birth is not simply beginning. It is continuous and continual beginning as such. And is it also the surging forth of this "as such," the interruption of the continuity of being that is always already begun and never-ending.

In the space-time of birth, the unattributeable immemorial of the real is retained and presented as such. The absolute takes place. If the *absolute* means what is absolutely detached from everything—the "me = me" that does not go beyond itself—then, each time there is a birth where something detaches and distinguishes itself, it is precisely the absolute that is born. The mystery of the absolute is raised in the smallest upheaval. Mystery raised: set upright, the female Sphinx, but also resolved, generously unveiled. Every mystery is a rising and a resolution.

> *Maria nursed her herself, and one day I saw her uncover her bosom and offer her breast.*
>
> *It was a plump, round bosom with brown skin and blue veins that appeared under that lustrous skin. At the time I had never seen a naked woman. Oh, the special ecstasy in which the sight of that breast plunged me! How I devoured it with my eyes, how I would like to have just touched that chest!*[48]

It is this extreme difficulty that makes life hard for us: that the mystery should turn out to be nothing mysterious at all, and that stripping it bare takes away nothing of its intimacy. This makes life hard for us, gives death its sting and makes philosophy ridiculous.

> *And you must cut this flesh from his breast,*
> *The Law allows it, and the Court awards it.*[49]

A world, yes, that is our question. But is it "world" or the "a" that should win out? Is "world" determined by unity? Or not?

To determine it in terms of multiplicity risks returning to the same. Multiple, multiplication of the one, originary reproduction, fold upon fold of one unique substance. By that reckoning the dual symmetry of the body—of so many bodies, animal, vegetable and mineral, mammalian and human—would be exemplary. But this is not true: the fold is not a dividing up of unity according to symmetry. It defies symmetry. From the moment there is plurality, there is incommensurability. There is incomparability in any pair. There is a difference between sides, like the difference between sexes. The right eye does not see like the left, and the left breast does not fall like the right. The perfectly duplicated bosom is a

bad image, caught in the grip of a metaphysics of fullness and completion—"twin globes" and other idiocies or obscenities.

There is neither unity nor multiplicity. There is the one and the other,
the one to the other, the one beside the other between the one and the
other.

Between the two a hollow, a wake, a fold opens up, offered through
the opening of a neckline, wide or narrow—*il canaletto*, as the Italians
say—but always a passage to another world, a point of access: access itself,
the pure notion of access.

Even when they are indistinguishable according to their properties, the
one and the other occupy different places in space. They oblige us to go
from one to the other. Synthesis is impossible. The a priori condition of
experience is the impossibility of synthesis, and the proof of that is offered
by the neckline.

Synthesis, or the position of the breast. There is a position that abandons, deposes the thing to itself. But there is also a position that imposes
a fantasy a priori: when Freud writes "I am the breast," he adds, "the
breast is a part of me." He does not give the "me" the chance to be part
of the breast. Still less did he allow both parties the chance to be in a
relation of *being* that would no longer be a matter of part and whole,
subsumption and absorption. It is a fantasy of identification achieved by
swallowing the nourishing body, itself reabsorbed into an organ, which
then becomes "part" of an omnipresent, devouring "all"—"me" suckling
on myself.

The situation is no better if the fantasy is of my being a part contained
within the breast:

> *that breast which already perhaps was bearing me in its shadowy taber-*
> *nacle a kind of gelatinous tadpole coiled around itself with its two enor-*
> *mous eyes its silkworm head its toothless mouth its cartilaginous insect's*
> *forehead, me?*[50]

always "me" and my birth or my death or my food or my beloved
partial object my part for my body or me self-worm in the body of the
other—whereas it is a matter of birth itself, long before me, self, you. It
is a matter of being born, dying: of being—not of coiling oneself around
so as to swallow oneself, choking oneself.

Then there is the fantasy where the object—the object fantasy—is the
disfiguring of the breast, a hallucination without tact or touch. How can
we talk of it with tact, and without swallowing it?

> *Can I suck your breast?*
> *Why do you like eating my breasts so much?*

I like the taste of them.
What do they taste like?
I don't know. Like nothing.
How about the taste of omelette with potatoes and onions?
That'd be great: one that tastes like omelette, the other like ham.[51]

It is a matter of trying to speak of an object that can't be made an object, one that is not in a relation of subjection with a subject. It is unsayable—because it arises in and with its being said.

The word. To say "breast"—or more to the point, sticking closer to the rhythm, to say "breasts"—tears at the heart, softly, and only so long as it, or they, are not said under conditions of anatomical, medical, or erotic super-objectivity, nor indeed under the condition of the subjectivity of mothering, between cradle and milk.

On the deck of Onassis' yacht, the Old Lion looked at Garbo "in a salacious way." Was she obliged to show him her breasts? The conquerors get the vanquished women. He will see what no one had ever seen.[52]

Something rises, sinuous without being insinuated. There is a seizure. Something ungraspable moves there in the chest and it is not a heart. The heart is only an elastic muscle beating according to a precise measure. The heart has no emotion. The proof: it can be changed; another one, all denerved and ready to function, can be transplanted in. But the breast cannot be grafted. It can be repaired, its wounds can be sewn up, it can be remodeled, but it is always itself, right down to the last scar.

Heart is a disheartening word. *Breast* is a weak word. It cannot, it can only be said badly.

It is not exactly an anatomical or descriptive term. It goes beyond that, no doubt like other terms such as *shoulder, neck, hip,* like these words for moving expanses, skin exposed, sagging, attentive to its own birth and to a hand that will come. Yet *breast* says more. It verges on prudishness, avoiding the embarrassment of coming too close to thighs or buttocks. It does not touch on obscenity or shame. It is the word for a shameless modesty that is also not indecent. It is a modesty that is proud of what it hides by exposing it.

Cowers, crossing her arms across her young breasts, holding them pressed against one another, one in each hand.[53]

Breast is a word that overflows and transfers to itself alone what it is supposed to name, just as the breast rises and in a certain way takes off the thing that is supposed to cover it. It is the lifting of its own veil and the relief of its own nudity.

Pure in subjects that are very pure, they will take
Sight, scent, taste, touch and hearing in God.
In the face of God will be our holy pleasures,
In the bosom of Abraham our desires will blossom,
Desires, perfect loves, high desires with no absence,
For fruit and flowers are born once only.[54]

Here there is no more transgression. There is no longer transgression, *strictly speaking*, if by *transgression* we mean violating a rule and crossing an uncrossable limit, penetrating into a sacred space. Perhaps there really is only transgression when there is rape: it is rape that institutes the forbiddenness of what it violates, because it violates it. It is what poses the proscription by mocking and breaking it. We see here an a priori structure of sacred separation and transgressive fault—the fault that falls beneath condemnation, or that it is the sacrificial impurity whose proper functioning constitutes redemption. (Heavy thoughts, twisted and morbid).

But the possibility of rape ends not with the beginning of prohibition or permission but with the beginning of proposition, disposition. This is why there is no rape where there is loving violence, falling somewhere between caress and blow, rhythm and jolt, tenderness and a slap. The body of love is suspended between what is offered and what is forbidden—or, to be more precise, what it forbids it nonetheless offers. But it is not a play of seductive and aggravating temptation; it is not a perverse invitation to be rebuked or even punished under the pretext of experiencing jouissance.

It is suspended between gift and refusal. It is not waiting for or in the power of either one. It is not in the grip of this gigantism of great, wild categories and sublime postures. It is something else. Gift and refusal belong to the order of exchange, and this can consist of an exchange of goods and services or hurts and harms. There is offer and request, and the offer itself is a request: the request that there be a request. But here it is something else. It is neither offer nor request—and as a result, in the end, not even offering. This word is still too religious, too sacrificial and too grandiloquent. Too intentional.

It is not about intention; it is about extension. It is a matter of what is tense without intention, offered without being requested, proposed without being invited.

I put my arms around him and drew him down to me so he could feel my breasts all perfume yes and his heart was going like mad and yes I said yes I will Yes.[55]

The breast waits for nothing, it promises nothing, it offers no exchange. It is seldom stripped bare either in painting or in fashion, rarely even proclaimed in its nudity, the birth of nudity, because it would be like a half-permitted nudity, half-transgressive, and thus set out front and in advance of a more withdrawn nude, more obscure and formidable, the one veiled by hair and hidden by the lips beneath their folds. If one nudity proclaims the other, it is not as a more deeply hidden secret or a more thoroughly forbidden darkness. It simply states complete nudity, from the hands and face right down to the most intimate humors of the body. The nude, or the soul. The soul is not an essence, it is a movement, a gesture, and an attraction.

There is volume, roundness, envelopment to which the hand is destined and, at the same time, the secret, intimacy, withdrawal into the depth of the valley. Nowhere does the body symbolize so much with itself, with the soul whose form it is.

> *Her dress announced the disorder of her mind: she wore around her neck a collar composed of the berries of eglantine. Her guitar was suspended upon her breast by a collar cord of ivy and withered fern; a white veil was thrown over her head and descended to her very feet.*[56]

> *Breast that would shame a rose; plump Breast,*
> *Of all things known, the loveliest;*
> *Firm Breast; indeed not Breast at all;*
> *Rather, a small, round ivory ball,*
> *And in the middle, a cherry placed,*
> *Or berry, and with such beauty graced*
> *That, though I neither touch nor see*
> *It bare, I vow such must it be.*[57]

X

On the Abuse of Nudity of the Bosom is the title of a work written by Abbé Jacques Boileau (brother of Nicolas Boileau) in the seventeenth century (a few years after the appearance of *Tartuffe*). In the nineteenth century, by contrast, we find a *Eulogy for Women's Breasts* by Mercier de Compiègne (a work hardly worth remembering).[58] The question is not whether these books and so many like them are ridiculous or naïve, insignificant or arrogant. What they do is make an object of what defies their censure or celebration, their desire or repression. They make an object: they make it commercial and ideal, a commodity and a fetish, creating symbolic use, symbolic value, and value as a plaything (symbol of a general symbolism, the breast of things, of nature or god, or even the plaything of an excited, voyeuristic, caressing jouissance). And yet, we still avoid the truth by setting these terms back to back (chests turned the other way): symbol and plaything, thing and fetish. It is as if we were not on the very verge of truth: the failure of intention and representation, the game as well as the symbol, the insignificance of sense, the embarrassment of abundance without abandon, and the birth of the infinite. *The divine child playing with dice*—and the Milky Way.

Ramón Gómez de la Serna (*Breasts*, 1917) knew something about this equivocation between the object and truth, which makes truth itself (1917: Europe had just breathed its last). The title withholds the article and so prevents breasts from becoming the object of representation. It attempts a bare offering of a bare semanteme (assuming also that the semanteme is plural). As if these things existed in language, that is, outside the dictionary—bare semantemes and radicals. As if it were possible to denude language. I must cite the point where his book wants to give up its secret because he knows very well that there is no secret to reveal, that everything is already there, and that even at the moment of beginning nothing more remained for him but the pain and pleasure of an irretrieveably fading writing, destined to waver between the picturesque and the metaphysical. Europe would end in a great flurry of activity, where sense drowned in detail, and vice versa. The loss of distinction—in order to distinguish what? the loss itself?

> *Breasts are the most malleable of man's secrets, and it is what I am desperately trying to divulge and express. Men have perhaps always been moved around the moment of incorporating themselves into breasts, waiting for those breasts, and even when they have been forgotten they have behaved like sleepwalkers at the feast of breasts. In the two hemispheres of the sphere which are breasts, the vanity of the earthly sphere appears. Damned be the mother of those who hypocritically abhor the naked, the mother who undressed before the father of those men, and whose nudity was the incentive for their birth. . . .*
>
> *Breasts are so definitive that when we think about the earth as if we had died, as if we had been definitively weaned, when we enter finally into the state in which one can no longer aspire to touch breasts, what we will most often see the others doing, those who remain, will be "playing with breasts." . . .*
>
> *The agitation and the first trembling, as if taking what belongs to another, perfectly of another being, of a being with its own life, of a being whose lovely sex does not correct or remedy or heal irremediable*

separation, this agitation and tremor is what occurs most in this work,
what constantly inserts itself in the text of this book and gives a certain
awkwardness to the words, the awkwardness and rapture one feels when
one welcomes new breasts for the first time. . . .

Will a moment come when clear eyes will see the lively chatter, that
bright and loquacious ensemble, that jabber of surprises that is in the
breasts? My quill has sought just that, and has thrown itself at it in
desperation.

The most sphinx-like aspect of the sphinx is not its smile or its eyes or
its face, but its breasts, its breasts, in which the secret of matter is con-
gealed as in no other form. [59]

Around the same time—a little earlier, in fact, fourteen years earlier,
fourteen years before the catastrophe, and who knows whether Gomez de
la Serna ever had the chance to read it?—a famous aesthetician, Theodor
Lipps, whose work Wilhelm Worringer, Max Scheler, and Freud all made
much use of, wrote a few pages on the feminine chest in his *Fundamentals
of Aesthetics.*

These pages occur in the exposition of his theory of *Einfühlung*, which
has been rendered in English—for the purpose of translating Lipps—as
"empathy," and in French as *empathie*. (The invention of these neolo-
gisms was a matter of transposing the Greek *empathès* into *Einfühlung*:
moved, affected, stirred, impassioned, subject to being moved, affected—a transposition in which the emphasis shifted to the *em-* (*ein-*) to
designate the capacity to feel in oneself what is endured, lived, or experienced in and by another.)

The question of empathy or whatever name we want to give it ("sympathy," "affective participation," "intropathy") was considered a cardinal
question in the first thirty years of the century. It was seen as the central
question of psychology and/or philosophy: it was understood as the question whose object would decide not only the particular register of affective
life, as well as that of communication in general and the knowledge of
others, but also the generic and fundamental register of the very possibility of thought, the register of the ontological or transcendental condition
of sense, and ultimately the register of the sense of sense, in all possible
senses.

How is there sense—that is to say, how is there truth for more than
one, shared truth? How does sense go, insofar as it goes from one to
another?

now I really am breathing and smelling nothing but her, who must have
felt, still sleeping, that I am smelling her and must not mind, because

she rises on her elbows, her face still held down, and from her armpit I move and smell what her breast is like, the tip.[60]

How is it that sense, before being the object of understanding, mistrust, or misunderstanding, is the subject of its own propagation among several? How is it that there is "for me" another "subject of sense"? Or how is sense the other subject for me and of myself, the subject other but with whom I nonetheless communicate, despite and in and across alterity, which is to say, above all, with whom I share the possibility of significance in general? How does sense introduce itself in person as such, before and across all signification, beyond or before every idea, everything eidetic and every idealization of sense, *logos* beyond all logic?

Hircus Civis Eblanensis! *He had buckgoat paps on him, soft ones for orphans. Ho Lord! Twins of his bosom. Lord save us! And ho!*[61]

For the beyond of sense in every sense and in all possible senses is not just a bottomless abyss where the irresistible vertigo of thought sinks under its own weight (not according to any mystical impulse but rather proceeding in the arid, restrained mode of an ascetic disciple pursuing an exact science). This beyond, or before—which does not hold anything in place and which has no place unless its place is always over there, in front—is just as much in the being alongside one another that we have all done from before birth, subjects, that is, subjected to sense: subjects of one another and all together, but separated, subjects of this sovereignty of sense,

Instantly, fleetingly, the everlasting future was manifest there, instantly mirror's light dipped into mirror's light. His hands lay upon her breasts, the points of which became harder under his touch—had she guided his hands?—and captured by the soft texture of her body, he heard Plotia say: "Beyond any poem is the unsung within you, greater than what is formed is that which forms; it forms you also, unattainably far from you, since it is your very self; yet when you draw near to me, you come near to this self and attain it." Not only her face, not only her breast took shape in his hands, nay, also her unseen heart nestling into the caressing embrace did so.[62]

which is not an empire; it dominates and governs nothing but yet, in some obscure way, we govern ourselves according to it, we, ourselves, one another with our makeshift radars. This beyond is in the contact and contagion by which we affect one another.

How then do we touch others, and how are we touched by them? Which is also to say: How are there others, since we are in the same sense, and there cannot possibly be others? How, then, if what touches us with the other—what puts us right at being *with* him/her—is not only and perhaps not at all what he/she feels, nor that he/she feels it, but this: for all that I feel it, it is the other as such that I feel in me, but the other *as such* in me is the other as other and this, he, she, cannot be in me. Being there nonetheless, being there as not being, like an outside inside, like an intruder.

> *we suggested a rapport to the telephone that could be reviewed from the perspective of the suckling, the telephone simultaneously as nipple and labia. . . . It is 1889; Bell . . . "discovered that these simple animals [sheep] had no teeth in their upper jaws, that they had—usually—one lamb at birth and that they suckled their young with two nipples. He was enchanted with these discoveries.". . . The sheep's minimal nipples, reduced to a pair, absorbs Bell's phantasmal energies. For Alexander Graham Bell the sheep take up a significance of affective investment of the same intensity as the telephone. He must multiply nipples. . . . Bell found that some of the sheep had an extra, rudimentary pair of nipples. And that one or two of the ewes habitually bore twin lambs. He satisfied himself that there was a connection between the supernumary mammae and the twins. . . . As enthusiastically as he had set out to contract space, as positively as he was to embark on the conquest of the air, Bell began to breed sheep to produce litters of lambs at birth. For thirty years Bell's labors over these breeding experiments was prodigious. . . . [It was a] phantasm of the reorganization of body parts in the movement from electric speech to the nipples of a sheep.*[63]

How can it be that I imitate neither the gestures nor expressions of others, but rather their very being-other, that is, their being-self? Their being turned on themselves in a way that makes them feel, and feel me too, and understand and suffer and experience jouissance? But what do we do, each one of us, when we say *I, like* everyone else?

It does not really matter that we have abandoned or at least neglected this approach to the question—the question of what makes us questioners. In fact, this approach remains entirely exterior. It assumes the "same" and the "other," the "proper" and the "stranger," in the very place where what is given—that which is given, "that" itself, where we are born, whence we are born—is quite anterior to these distinctions and much deeper than them. That is to say, it is much more dispersed, thrown across the world like a network with innumerable branches, a network of which all our cybernetic and digital connections are only a thinly traced line, soon rendered obsolete.

Democritus and Epicurus say the embryo in the womb is nourished through the mouth. Hence as soon as it is born it goes to the breast with its mouth. For in the womb too are nipples and orifices through which it is nourished.[64]

It does not really matter that we no longer state this question as such, since the affirmation that precedes and goes beyond it is even more severe, demanding, intractable. Being with one another, being delivered over to one another so much than we are delivered over to ourselves, this propels us toward a strange entanglement with the with: distance is opened up but prevented from being merely distance; it is proximity too, shy and intimidated. A long and heavy debate with ego-ity and egoism have left us an altered ego: but where does its thirst come from, and how come it cannot quench it?

Concordia discors: the heart of another with mine—how am I to hold them together in my chest? How gradually erase the scar without ever quite making it disappear, the scar of the incision through which, by sawing and opening up my ribcage, they got it in there?

Deep stereoscopic regard. To see double. Two columns, two hills, two breasts. It is impossible. The colpos *between the one and the two.*[65]

How are we to know others? This is a false question, since "others" are already given in knowledge in general; there is nothing or no one I know without relating it to something other than itself. The notion that it is possible to know in general, to know some thing or other, that is to say, the thought that it is possible to relate something to some principle or reason, to some model or identity, this itself assumes that the principle or model, reason or identity are already shared, recognizable to us. This in turn assumes some feeling of this sharing and recognition. (Which then assumes, as Kant says, some originary, forgotten pleasure in knowledge as such.)

Such a feeling is experienced with others—which is to say that it is the feeling of the "with" itself, which in the end is nothing other than the possibility of feeling, of being touched, of being susceptible to affection. In order to be affected one must be affectable, and to be affectable one must be exposed and not just posed. What is needed is a condition of exteriority, of opening, and passivity or vulnerability that is more ancient than everything else.

yes I think he made them a bit firmer sucking them like that so long he made me thirsty titties he calls them I had to laugh yes this one anyhow stiff the nipple gets for the least thing Ill get him to keep that up and Ill

*take those eggs beaten up with marsala fatten them out for him what
are all those veins and things curious the way its made 2 the same in
case of twins theyre supposed to represent beauty placed up there like
those statues in the museum* [66]

Not a mark or an originary imprint but, on the contrary, a passive
power to be marked, imprinted, impregnated, what is known as "being
impressionable," that is, being susceptible to receiving a strong impression
in the presence of something that is not necessarily all that impressive. To
be sensitive is to be receptive to what hardly makes itself felt at all. The
measure of sense is the infinitesimal, that which goes to the limit. It is a
matter of approaching a limit where sensibility itself is moved, that is,
receives itself in itself from what is infinitely outside of it, infinitely light.

*Her bosom is small, set a little low like the bosom of a pregnant woman,
but it is firm and, above all, has a tendency to quiver.*[67]

*He asked her to disrobe and she did so, but slowly. The doctor's hands
were skillful and deft but her breasts were already sore from the machine
and as he prodded and squeezed and manipulated and flattened her
flesh the woman bit her lip to keep from crying out.*[68]

XI

When Theodor Lipps analyzes *empathy* in relation to the bodies of others,
in an effort to arrive at an instinctive imitation of movements or postures,
he adds this consideration:

> *The instinctive impulses toward movement that we are describing here
> are nevertheless only ever impulses toward movement in the narrow
> sense, that is, impulses whose functioning gives rise to bodily movement,
> or would give rise to such movement.*
>
> *But in the end there are also forms for which such impulses toward
> movement mean nothing. I am thinking here of the forms of the female
> torso; I mean the forms that are specific to the female torso. Here the
> theory of imitation clearly fails completely. No motor neurons produce
> or change these forms. And the forms are quite strange to me, a man. It
> is quite impossible for me to experience in myself the life that is played
> out in these forms. I am also incapable of "recreating" that life within
> myself.*
>
> *Every explanation on the basis of experience also fails here. There is
> only one way to think of this, one that I will later use in other cases. It
> could be said that the forms in question belong just to the female body;*

they are a part of this living whole and take part in its life. They are experienced as cooperating in the whole life of the female body. And thus insofar as this life is enjoyed, they are beautiful.

But two different objections arise here. First, for many of us, the opportunity to observe these female forms and to verify how they belong to the whole of the body presents itself far too seldom. Second, the forms in question are not beautiful in all circumstances; they can even be quite ugly. And undoubtedly beautiful forms are the exception rather than the rule. For the most part, it is the ugly forms that must appear as belonging to the whole body and thus as beautiful.

Maybe it seems easy to find another way here. We can always refer to the sexual instinct. The habit of dragging it into aesthetics seems to have become something of a fashion, one that is very much of a piece with our contemporary ethical—and therefore also aesthetic—decadence. In opposition to this fad, I will take this opportunity to state that the sexual has nothing—nothing at all—to do with the aesthetic. Those who use it to explain aesthetic sentiment know as little about the meaning of beauty and aesthetic contemplation as those who object to "nudity" in art because they fear the dangerous effect of chaste nudity on morals: their own, first of all but, insofar as they project their own crudity onto others, on the morality of others, too.[69]

In fact, the forms in question owe their beauty to empathy, as all forms do. And this has nothing in common with the sexual instinct. For that, the specific forms of the opposite sex are the object of a possible real relationship. It is a question of knowing what the forms mean, not for the individual to whom they belong, but for me, who stands over against this individual as another individual, specifically, one belonging to the other sex. In empathy, by contrast, the question is what the forms mean for the I who have them, how I feel about them. It is certainly not a matter of my understanding but of my own sentiment. Or—and it amounts to the same thing—what sense I have of myself, that is, the life I live when I can identify with the individual I perceive when, through contemplation, I linger and become quite absorbed in her and in the forms of her body, leaving completely out of the question my own I, above all my sexually differentiated I, which stands facing her.

In short, when it comes to the aesthetic contemplation of human bodies, and insofar as the difference between man and woman is a sexual difference that can be sensed and not a difference in character or temperament, I am simply neither man nor woman. I am no more a sexually differentiated individual than I am a farmer when I contemplate a landscape aesthetically, or a lumberjack or a carpenter when I contemplate a tree aesthetically.

Therefore, the aesthetic contemplation of female forms is—or can be—the same for a woman as it is for a man, and vice versa.

This is not rooted in the sense of aesthetic empathy alone. It is, rather, the experience of anyone who has ever contemplated the human form aesthetically. I sense in beautiful female bodies a strange, healthy, powerful, swelling, blooming life; I have a sense of physical well-being that cannot be localized anywhere but in the form I perceive. It is a sense of well-being that I cannot have, given who I am, that is, given that I am a man. It is something granted to me only in the act of aesthetic contemplation. It is a case of enriching my pleasure in life above and beyond my actual I.

And it is immediately clear and certain to me that my sense of beauty is just this. In the aesthetic contemplation of these forms I find myself looking right through the forms and seeing the life that is proper to them, and then I experience growing in me a sense of happiness that I have otherwise never known. I have characterized this as a sense of "physical well-being." What I mean by this is not something that the body experiences but rather a particular pleasure in self and life, comparable to that given to me in the course of my bodily life and that, for this reason, I relate or attach to my body and my bodily life.

Besides, this sentiment arises where every sentiment occurs, namely, in the soul, and, like every sentiment, its immediate cause is a psychic event. Every sentiment is the expression of a consciousness, or a phenomenon accompanying a particular mode of the course of psychic life. The perceived form then determines the course of my psychic life as I contemplate it, as I give myself over to contemplation of it. It communicates impulses to this psychic life, giving it a particular rhythm; these are impulses and a rhythm that I experience in these forms, that I sense in the forms themselves. . I have said more precisely above that what I sense through empathy in these particular forms is power, health, and swelling, blooming life. By that I meant power and health that can be sensed, life that is sensed. And yet I can feel only what is psychic. Bodily states, the "rhythms" of bodily life can be sensed by me only insofar as they become psychic, or insofar as they determine the course of my psychic life, giving power, vivacity, richness, and freedom to my psychic existence.

What are impulses like, independent of my sentiments? I have no idea. I have them only as sentiment. But in any case, they are not the same as those I experience once I leave aesthetic contemplation behind, once I stop lingering contemplatively over forms and instead situate my-self vis-à-vis them as a matter of my sexual difference. In brief, these impulses are something other than the drives of sexual instinct.

This also must be added: I sense in the forms I perceive the rhythm that is particular to the course of the life of my soul. It doesn't matter whether the one to whom the forms belong feels the same thing.

The facts of the matter as I have laid them out are relatively new to us. One can find there a new broadening of the principle that explains to us the beauty of human forms. We now see that the forms we perceive visually do not just awake in us the impulse to imitate, that is, to under-take movements that would produce in another the same visual image. Nor do they only awaken impulses toward movements that would ex-ploit the forms I perceive. Rather, they bring about, in a general man-ner, psychic impulses; they set in motion a mode of psychic life. Those impulses toward movement are impulses through which the psyche aims at an effect by means of a distinct bodily process. They are also, in a mediated fashion, impulses toward a mode of inner being or a type of comportment, knowledge out of which this sort of impulse naturally arises, and with which they make up a psychic whole. Now we see that the impulses springing from the visual perception of bodily forms may also be unmediated impulses toward just such a mode of inner comport-ment or course of psychic life.

By establishing the specificity of these impulses, we have, as I have already stated, distanced ourselves completely from the concept of imita-tion that for a while seemed to satisfy us. I imitate nothing when I con-template the female form. I do not seek to reproduce a process, but in the contemplation of the forms—and only in that contemplation—there arises spontaneously a mode of living activity that seems to be bound up with the forms. This case shows more clearly than any other the distinc-tion between the concepts of empathy and imitation.[70]

Of course, it is not a question of undertaking a critical analysis of this text, which would first of all require setting it in its historical and theoreti-cal context. Despite its distance from us, and despite its deep confusions, it communicates a curious fascination: it tries to give an account of the very thing that it undergoes. Women's breasts represent the paradigmatic case of identification as opposed to imitation. (Note that it is a matter of women's breasts for men and not for women. Only man has the opportu-nity or the need for identification.)

If I had breasts I'd fondle them all day long.[71]

Identification is the possibility of being transported into the other, that is, of a relation to the other that does not hold it at a distance, like an object, nor even at the distance of another subject, but that frees the subject of its differentiated (in this case, sexual) identity in order to identify, not with another subject, but with what the other merely bears—which Lipps calls the exuberance of life itself, as the intensification, in principle limitless, of life as the feeling of self.

Originary identification, at the very origin, with the exuberance of the origin. Exuberance is the overflowing of what flows in abundance from the breast—*uber*. It is the gushing of a flood that surpasses all measure (*exundat et exuberat illa eloquentia*, that abounding and overwhelming eloquence, Tacitus said) or a superabundant fecundity (*pomis exuberat annus*, the year abounding in fruit, Virgil wrote). (Lipps uses the word *Schwellen*, swelling, dilation, flood, erection.) *Uber* comes from the same root as the Greek *uthar*, the Sanskrit *udhar*, from which come the German *Euter* and the English *udder*. But the breast of identification is not the mammalian organ; it is the exuberance of life itself.

(In Latin, *ubera* sometimes takes on the sense of *amores*.)

> *whereas this could not be said of Ann's chest, that it was weak, whatever might be said of other parts of her, for it is well known that Ann had a splendid bosom, white and fat and elastic, and what could be more natural, in the mind of a man like Jack, weak-minded and tied to a weak-chested woman, than that the thought of this splendid part of Ann, so white, so fat, and so elastic, should grow and grow, whiter and whiter, fatter and fatter, and more and more elastic, until all thought of those other parts of Ann (and they were numerous) where whiteness did not dwell, nor fatness, nor elasticity, but greyness, and even greenness, and thinness, and bagginess, were driven quite away.*[72]

Identification with what identifies but remains without identity for itself, without an identical. Breasts: breasts, each time simply breasts.

> *And the eyes, like precious stones, are not worth this look that comes from her happy flesh: breasts raised up as if they were full of an eternal milk, the point towards the sky, with smooth legs that guard the salt of the first sea.*[73]

> *Her swimming was full of a sort of ecstatic delight; and lapped by the ripples, shivering with a sensuous joy, she rose with every stroke as if she would spring out of the river. . . . Then, slackening speed, she turned over abruptly and floated, with her arms crossed and her eyes lost in the blue of the sky. He gazed at her stretched thus on the surface of the water, at the curving lines of her body, her bosom firm and round under*

the stuff of the clinging gown, her half-submerged thighs, her bare shins gleaming through the water, her little feet peeping out.[74]

Exuberance, overflowing, full, spurting, flowing, flow.

Mastos, "the breast" in Greek, comes from a root that means humidity. In Sanskrit, *madati* is a wet or drunk being, like *madeo* in Latin. Being wet, damp, streaming, full of fluid. Sometimes *mastos* means a drinking cup in the form of a breast. They say that Helen offered Athena a cup molded on her own breast.

> *. . . by the two breasts of Tellus*
> > *Bless my buttons, a staff car/*
> *si come avesse l'inferno in gran dispitto*
> *Capanaeus*
> > *with 6 on 3, swallow-tails*
> *as from the breasts of Helen, a cup of white gold . . .*[75]

Wetness molded, plastic, presented. The flood or flux grasped, offered in the form of a wave. Aristotle said that the wet gives shape to the dry. The dry is the hard, unmoving heart of things, a point of being that is flung into the middle of nothingness. There is a raising of being that bursts forth and falls back, but no point or fold, that which lifts them up, coming, hardly staying, abundance that bends, abandoned for a palm or a mouth. *Thēlē,* "the teat" in Greek, is what abounds and flowers, the luxuriance of plants, flourishing life.

> *Regarded as a martyr,*
> *A little nipple that sighs,*
> *That swells, stands up proudly*
> *Lifting the sheet a good two inches.*
> *A hand reaches and closes upon*
> *The best-loved thigh*
> *And in between the breasts*
> *Another white hand finds its place.*
> > *. . .*
> *My girl shows her hip*
> *And a little of her thigh*
> *Whiter than lilies, snow, satin*
> *And in the morning her breasts*
> *Have gone beyond the end of her bed.*[76]

Thelus is feminine, tender, delicate, soft, fruitful. The root is **dhe*—fruitfulness, lactation, with the action of sucking, nursing. From there comes *felare*, "to suck" and *fecondus*, and *felix, femina* or *filius*. But "to suck," *sugare* in Latin, comes in its turn from another root—**seu*—for humidity, rain, juice. The Greek *hyle*, the forest, may come from there too, and thus also wood as material and material in general, as Aristotle presupposes it and opposes it to form, *morphē*.

Form and matter: nothing but their joint belonging, in advance of any distinction.

> *the tangible presence (perfume, breathing, warmth, patches of white flesh, density) of breasts and thighs and hips which with the same glee, the same calm sentiment of victory, he had only to stretch out his hand to touch, to feel under the thin kimonos, able to see in the wan light from the two bulbs the jade-green shadow which ran like paint out of a tube from the delicate turn of the neck down to where the lapels of the kimono began to separate, widening, slipping over the naked flesh made, apparently, of some translucent paste, its sinuous and shifting contour changing with each breath, insinuating itself like a liquid stream be-tween the two parts of the light garment decorated with leaves and fruits, apricot, red, orange.*[77]

Matter is nothing but the consistency of form, which in turn is nothing but the finishing of matter. They cling to one another, each one the bearing and coming of the other. Impenetrability and visibility of the one to the other. Matter is form flowing according to its own substance. Form is matter sucked according to its own essence.

> *that singular object—which I am trying to unstick in your minds from the food metaphor—the breast. The breast is also something superim-posed, who sucks what?—the organism of the mother.*[78]

> *The points of her proud breasts lifted the cloth of her mauve-pink tunic, creating two folds that could have been carved in marble by Phidias or Cleomenes.*[79]

XII

Presentation itself—its fading away.

> *The tiger springs towards the two martyrs. He raises himself up, and burying his nails in the body of the son of Lasthenes, he tears away, with his teeth, the shoulders of the intrepid confessor. As Cymodocea, still pressed against the breast of her husband, opens upon him her eyes*

*filled with love and terror, she perceives the tiger's blood-stained head
near the head of Eudorus.*[80]

The rhythm of being—or, rather, being itself as rhythm. The sense of being, as they say. Raised up, beating, beaten, fallen, cadence. Resistance, abandon. Birth, ascent, separation of the two sides of a united, gently divided body. Areality: neither thing nor person, neither subject nor object, but between the two—

—identification itself, like the eye that has no vision of a sameness that is differently disposed, indefinitely different—an insubstantial substance, desire without lack, the tendency of a naked nature toward ever more nudity but not toward any secret, and not by means of any transgression. In full bloom, maybe overblown, young or old, bloated or flabby, this nudity is the same, always at the conjunction:

*. . . there is nothing I do not dream
there is nothing I do not cry*

*further than tears, death
higher than the ground of the sky*

in the space of your breasts . . .[81]

*And I have seen the human phallus,
the beating of Cecile's heart between her breasts
in this groove in the rack of bones
where the soul to be confirmed smells the dead woman.*[82]

—because there must be disjunction and separation, but not because there is incompleteness or lack or finitude, as they say, but simply because nothing has value all on its own.

*For Andromeda, the lightning of your kisses.
Your virginal veils and your lover's languor,
And the slow sigh of your narrow breasts,
Faithless Atthis!* [83]

Why is it so difficult to make oneself understood? So much more difficult than the bitterness and melancholy of being-alone, which maybe says nothing else?
We never know where or when the knowledge . . .
All elegance is of . . .

*The gaze—(conversation)—the touch of hands—the kiss—the contact
of breasts—the grasping of sexual parts—the embrace—these are the*

steps of the ladder—on which the soul raises itself—this ladder is the opposite of that on which the body raises itself—to the point of the embrace. Feeling—perceiving—possessing.[84]

—always at the conjunction of the other and the same, always at this confusion of identity that is more powerful than identity because one must be a little beside oneself in order to be to oneself, always beside, never there, never other, never the same.

An immemorial immobility is shaken, the immobility of a bust or a sacred torso, the sculpture that is the monument and ruin of the origin, hands crossed in front of the impassive marble chest of a divinity that has no face, no abyss, no secret, no breath, no emotion. It is the movement in place of almost nothing.

I am a wall, and my breasts like towers: then was I in his eyes as one that found peace.[85]

Birth, upheaval, inclination, incline: identification with nothing but the unidentifiable, with a shock that spreads imperceptibly, that gathers force and feeds on itself, perceptible imperceptibility. We cannot distinguish between a joy and a pain, between one accent and another. It comes and is lost, passion, compassion—equivocating between the two.

This is how we reach truth: by turning it away from itself in order to observe its silence, breathing, and birth. There is truth, for I am not alone and this moves beside me, before me.

The passion of knowing, compassion of not knowing. Pushed simultaneously toward contact and toward what is intact. The emotion of what is hidden in the organized body and what is incorporated in the neighboring body, always neighboring. Novelty at every turn, every joint, the unforeseeable rise of a cheek, a hip, a palm or bosom. The unknown toward which this rises and moves.

Thus the breast: matter itself, exuberance, elevation, presentation, identity, decay, birth absolutely—but detached, distinct, carried before itself, birth set apart like a part of being, the autonomous part of autonomy itself, independence depending on nothing but itself, falling suspended raised upright heavy light, in fact another body, organ without body, disorganized body, madly isolated and stimulated, apart, offered and hidden, twice, always twice, sweet balance.

Thought is reached by rising as such, without appeasement—because "as such" is at no point like itself, never as such. The agitation of thought—its unbearable susceptibility to being itself and to truth, birth, death, and being beside—comes from its deep taste for the emotion that gives birth to it, and it matters to it more than anything else that it should melt into it in a single trace, supple and divisible.

It shows up here like this: since what first appeared as the object sinks for consciousness to the level of its way of knowing it, and since the in-itself becomes a being-for-consciousness *of the in-itself, the latter is now the new object. Herewith a new pattern of consciousness comes on the scene as well, for which the essence is something different from what it was at the preceding stage. It is this fact that guides the entire series of the patterns of consciousness in their necessary sequence. But it is just this necessity itself, or the* origination *of the new object, that presents itself to consciousness without its understanding how this happens, which proceeds for us, as it were behind the back of consciousness. Thus in the movement of consciousness there occurs a moment of* being-in-itself *or* being-for-us *which is not present to the consciousness comprehended in the experience itself. The content, however, of what presents itself to us does exist* for it; *we comprehend only the formal aspect of that content, or its pure origination. For it, what has thus arisen exists only as an object; for us, it appears at the same time as movement and a process of becoming.*[86]

The difficulty is overwhelming because the identity of becoming, which is a matter of being touched by an apprehension that follows the contour of the movement of the thing itself, has no presence other than that of its curve, which precedes it infinitely according to the progress of an emergence from self—that is, from nothing. This is why consciousness sees nothing and discerns nothing of this and so takes on the very movement that skirts around it and passes it by.

Yvonne was sitting up half reading her magazine, her nightgown slightly pulled aside showing where her warm tan faded into the white skin of her breast, her arms outside the covers and one hand turned downward from the wrist hanging over the edge of the bed listlessly: as he approached she turned this hand palm upward in an involuntary movement, of irritation perhaps, but it was like an unconscious gesture of appeal: it was more: it seemed to epitomize, suddenly, all the old supplication, the whole queer secret dumb show of incommunicable tendernesses and loyalties and eternal hopes of their marriage.[87]

But what happens in the back of consciousness, so to speak—"so to speak" because it has no back, it has no thickness, it is itself only its point reaching toward the contact of experience—what happens there that is itself for us before us: in front of us, both coming to meet us and at the same time preceding us, we who are not consciousness but who are thought itself, that is to say, the refolding of being in the upheaval of its birth, the taking back into itself of all its outside—this birth that, as a result, *is* not, or *is not born* except for us, and not, for all that, according to some relation or intentionality but *right at* us and as this "we," according to our rhythm which is the rhythm of being born itself and of being only being born, infinitely infinitesimally rising before us, us before ourselves like a heart-breaking softness that incomprehensibly opens our night to still more night, opening the universe to its proper curvature refolded everywhere and everywhere reopened, traversed in all senses by a network of fine veins and long trails of galaxies.

The point of view of thought is the blind seeing whose tears flow, whose laughter flows, in the bosom of this immense outside.

> *If night is falling and the carriage is moving fast, whether in town or country, there is not a single torso, disfigured like an antique marble by the speed that tears us away and the dusk that blurs it, that does not aim at our heart, from every crossing, from the lighted interior of every shop, the arrows of Beauty, that Beauty of which we are sometimes tempted to ask ourselves whether it is, in this world, anything more than the complementary part that is added to a fragmentary and fugitive stranger by our imagination, overstimulated by regret.*[88]

> *This notion of calm comes from him. Without him I would not have had it. Now I'll wipe out everything but the flowers. No more rain. No more mounds. Nothing but the two of us dragging through the flowers. Enough my old breasts feel his old hand.*[89]

> *But the Egyptian, her breasts bared, sits*
> *And goes on singing, her joints gouty with grief,*
> *In the woods, by the fire.*[90]

Paean to Aphrodite

(Divine one, sing me the foam, the crest and pearl of the waves on the wine-dark sea, and that song of love that has washed your lips, and also the one that stays on the lips of the singer, the song over, the myth dispersed.)

(Another song? You said it yourself: the voices have been silenced.

—That's true, but that's why I say: sing me what's left.

—But there's nothing left.

—That's true too. But I tell you, sing me nothing, the foam.

—That's too easy.

—Admit then that it's too difficult, and well you know it.

—No, I don't know.

—Then don't sing, foam.)

Aphrodite, born of the foam: that is what her name means, *Aphrodite aphrogeneia* according to what is known as popular etymology, gathered by Plato in his *Cratylus*. Of course, nobody believes it, and Plato reports it with a smile. But Aphrodite is "the one who likes a smile" or "the one who smiles willingly." Is that what the blind singer calls her: *Aphrodite philommeides*?

(Hesiod calls her *philommedes*, "the one who loves the shaft": Which word hides which? Which smiles from behind the other?)

The plains of the sea smile at you, *tibi rident aequora ponti*. Lucretius also says, on the threshold of his poem: you alone govern the nature of things, *rerum naturam sola gubernas*.

The government of things begins with a smile from the *etymon*: a smile from the true, the original. It is not a matter of derision or parody—just a smile. The pretenders to the *etymon* in this case are many: there is *Astarte*, and *Prytanis*, lord, *fruit, tyrant, Phrygian*, and we find here also something Etruscan and Semitic, something of the Aegean and of everything that still begins by losing itself, by blending itself with the contours, agitations, and depths of the sea of so many Peripluses, this sea between so many lands.

The name is also expressed by this epithet or nickname: *anadyomene*, who surges from the depths, who rises again or, more precisely, plunges toward the heights, penetrating and rising. The goddess inverts the sense of depth. In her, depth becomes surface; *makes itself* surface, it rises and is carried off by the foam at the foot of the rock of Paphos in Cyprus. It is not Aphrodite who rises from the abyss, it is the abyss that rises in her.

And why not, since she governs things, since it is she who makes their primitive comings, *rerum primordia, semina rerum*, the elements of all that exist, all the atoms, all their seminal, disseminal falls, atomic Aphrodite?

ॐ

(Do you hear the words I am saying? Do you know that for us they are words of war and sorrow?)

ॐ

There is no hidden god. Here there is nothing hidden about the divine, nothing mysterious or secret. Depth rises to the surface, to the surfaces. This is not about mysteries, or theologies or philosophies. *Aphros* has to do with clouds (*abhra* in Sanskrit), but this cloud does not obscure anything, it does not dissimulate anything at all. It is every bit as much the clearness of the sky touched by water. It is the clearness of the sky washed by foam.

This very clear point, this blend of sky and water, is the place where the gods are laid bare, when there are no more gods.

Of course the *etymon* of *foam* ["*écume*"] is also that of *obscure* ["*obscur*"] but here *etymon* and depth are both reversed. *Anetymology*: sense is not deep down, behind, before; it is right at the surface; it pushes it toward nudity.

Aphrodite is naked for all the gods.

~3~

The surface is not laid upon a depth: it is depth that appears and makes a whole surface. The foaming surface is birth itself; she is the goddess who is born and who is divine only by virtue of being born like this, on the crest, in the frill of each wave and in the spreading foam of each trough.

The birds of the air celebrate you and your coming, divine one. *Aeriae volucres te, diva, tuumque significant initum.*

Meanwhile, this manifestation of the abyss does not set anything up above the foam. Aphrodite is not deep but, standing erect on the sea and reaching the sky, she is also not a beacon or a phallus. Penetration does not light up the sea, it does not probe it: it only wets, foams, is wetted; it is the sea distilling its marine essence. Aphrodite deceives straining, priapic love that comes on too strong. She is the deception of knowledge. She does not hold up the sky of Ideas. (Euripides and Plato revive the practice of distinguishing Uranian Aphrodite from Pandemonian Aphrodite, but taken apart like that, what is left of her?) She touches only the foam. She is the touch of the foam.

Yet this is not to say that the phallus is suppressed. Nor is it a matter of castration. It is not the story of Uranus; the foam is no more sperm than it is all of the fluids and liquids of love.

And yet this is the story of Uranus: Aphrodite was born of the sea after it was impregnated by the blood of his severed genitals. Diogenes of Apollonia called sperm *aphros haimatos*, the foam of blood. *Exaphroun*: blood turned to foam, aphrohemorrhage, alchemy, *menstruum universale*. It is the effervescence of the sky in the water, the sea mixed with sun, and it is not a mutilation.

There is the story of Attis, his phallus cut for Cybele-Astarte, the Good Goddess, Idaean mother of the mountains, the great Mother of Syria. But a jet of foam dissolves stone blades as well as bronze ones and there is no sacrifice. Waves wash the mountain, and nothing is cut off when one sex passes through the other.

Philommedes, philomeides, forever unresolved. The story is always different. It is the story of the metamorphosis, where each difference imprints its different mark on the other. Each one goes into the other beyond self and other and neither comes back to itself or loses itself. Never identifiable and never clearly distinct, the truth in a soul and a body.

Aphrodite offers the phallus along with the foam. In its cult it is presented with a grain of salt. Neither knowledge nor myth can understand anything of this offering. *Phallus,* not only wet but wetness itself, foam, nothing but salty foam. The first idols of the Great Goddess of Cyprus are of indeterminate sex. Aphrodite herself occasionally becomes Aphroditos. Rather than a couple made up of phallus and excision, this is the doublet of the penile and penis, our common hermaphrodite, which has no *etymon* to support it.

Aphrodite twice over: female, male, without mixture or confusion. Divided, multiplied, shared from the start, with no common measure. The differential calculus of the unlimited limit of a double touch. From top to bottom, from bottom to top, sex—a cutting name—splits Aphrodite in a way that mutilates nothing. From one part to the other, from one intact foam to the other—the charm and chance of tact.

The name *Aphrodite* is by no means the only name and the only divine name whose provenance is twisted, disputed, driven out to sea, floating between the waters. But it is perhaps the only one whose smiling *etymon* indicated just that: pitching and rolling, crests and rollers, the swell and spray of waves, moving in place first this way, then that, roiling surf, lapping water, streaming wake. Marine Aphrodite, Aphrodite the Navigator, *pontia, euploia Aphrodite.*

၃

(Paean, your strophes are useless; you give us a froth of words, a sparkling wine, but the party is over, Don Giovanni, the music committed to memory. The infinite melody is lost in the fog, and the ritornello turns around and around. We are overwhelmed. Your froth leaves us disheartened; we can only fall silent. Aphrodite is sad today.)

၃

What corresponds to the shining foam is the sparkling of the star: Ashtoreth, mother of Baal, planet Venus, going and coming, Innana of Sumeria, Ashtart, Ishtar of Babylon or Nineveh, who speaks with the Great Wave of the Sea, Hathor of Egypt, the cow with the lyre-shaped horns that carry the sun, Esther, the Jew, bathed for a whole year in myrrh and aromatic herbs for the king whose anger she finally deflects. *Planet Aphrodite*, goddess of going astray, from one people to another, from feast to feast, name to name, under the errant signs in the sky: *caeli subter latentia signa*. Goddess of that for which there is no god.

Evening and morning star, Hesper and Lucifer, star of the shepherd, rising and setting here and there, coming and going in the arms of Ares, Dionysus, Hermes, Anchises, Adonis, or Attis, mother of Harmony, Eros, and Anteros, Deimos and Phobos, Aeneas, Hermaphrodite, and then standing naked before Paris, silently, by her very silence, promising him Helen. Great Mother and also a girl who gets around, Homer, Flaubert, Freud, and Offenbach.

Paean, Song of Songs, "you are beautiful, my beloved": this was sung in Jerusalem in honor of Ishtar and Tammuz-Adonis. Later, despite Jeremiah's anger, Astarte was offered cakes in the form of the naked goddess. Was King Sargon of Accad not set adrift on the water, like Moses, and rescued by Ishtar?

Aphrodite, pantheon of the billows, pandemonium of foam; it is a stream in flood, but it cherishes no gnosis, no secret knowledge of deliverance.

(Like us?

—Yes, like us.

—No more deliverance, no more salvation, no more belief?

—Indeed, no more reason to rejoice in it, any more than to lament its passing.)

Neither knowledge nor wisdom but beauty. Plato should reunite Urania and Pandemos in the impulse of Eros. Beauty passes from bodies to souls—and how will the souls stop asking for bodies again, asking to pass into them in order to be beautiful? Aphrodite is the passage. The cortege comes and goes between the two temples of Urania, one with the statue of Phidias and the other with the statue of Alcmene, and the temple of Pandemos where Solon set up official prostitution.

(Strabon says that all the women of Babylon, in obedience to some divine precept, would have sex with foreigners in the temple of Aphrodite, ceremonially and in the midst of the crowd. The money poured out by the foreigners was consecrated to the service of the goddess. They paid for breasts smeared with honey and thighs rubbed with myrtle and aloe.)

Urania is exclusively masculine, and Pandemos proceeds from the two sexes. But what does Eros do except put the one in the other, and in every possible way? How can Aphrodite divide the sexes? She is nothing but their division and sharing in one another, between one another. Aphrodite is one in two, not two in one. Not "bisexed" (we are not talking about a pulmonary gastropod), but one in two sexes—and in such a way that there is no one without two and, finally, there is no one. No one sex is one. No one Aphrodite is one. *Aphrodite androgynos.* Always naked for all the gods, for both of them.

Plato kept his distance. He preferred Eros. He made him not her son but the offspring—born the same day as she was—of two laborious concepts. Needy love, *Eros philosophos*: twin brother of the foam, withdrawn onto the dryness of thought. The dry and solid soil where one can build solidly, durably.

But Plato-Friend-of-Ideas is not finished with the sex-that-has-no-idea. He goes looking for a philosophical Aphrodite and finds her in Diotima of Mantinea. We do not know who she is. A fiction? The memory of a Pythagorean? Or a priestess of the Lycian Zeus? It does not matter. She says the knowledge of beauty. But, in order for Aphrodite to survive, do we need a beautiful wise woman? Who knows how beautiful Diotima was? Not knowing drove Hölderlin mad.

Diotima hides behind Socrates, whose ugliness protects real Beauty. Nevertheless, Plato loved beauty, more than he could say. Thus Diotima, the only Plato-woman, Socrates in drag, made up, beautiful at last, invades our memories in her absence.

But why does poetry never release its hold on us? Since everything is ugly, it remains more than a memory. Why is it immemorial and without history? Why does Plato want beautiful discourse?

᷾

(Paean, beautiful thought, sing no more, let your flute players fall silent and tell me the law of this "powerful Aphrodite whose insubordination is so well known." *Ataktos Aphrodite*, what is her order, her rule, her immeasurable measure? Say it to me if you can, say the sentence of such a thought. Say this naked sentence to me, aphasic Aphrodite.)

᷾

Aphrodite. Her name is born of a foam of words, from the foam of words: sense that is perfectly proper, sense ideally appropriated by games, by a figure with long tresses, a fiction soaking wet, streaming with this love of words, of senses, of this inalterable impropriety of languages that ravishes and deceives us by turns and in equal parts, the coming and going that carries us and carries us off.

(One could just as easily say: Aphrodite comes from Africa, aphorism, afraid, afforest, afresh. And it is clear that this would not be to say something false. All of it makes up an *etymon*: studied properly, all foam etymologizes [*toute écume étyme*].)

Come from elsewhere and everywhere, daughter of islands and coasts, she sends the Greeks to sea, sets Helen, who is pursued by all the Kings, on board ship. Wounded by the game she set in motion, she makes her dear Trojans set sail, Anchises on Aeneas's back, unable to return to the East, reaching the shores of the West, *Aenaedum genetrix*, mother of Aeneas's race.

She displaces and mixes up principles, harmony, pleasure, and force. She seduces origins, carrying far afield the peoples who have come from afar, carrying their unknown origins, temporary foundations, inventions, momentary convulsions, wakes traced, palaces and golden peacocks, villas. Her real temple is the foaming City, filled with innumerable temples, hidden passages, comings and goings. And yet, with the same rhythm of triremes heavy with slaves and goods, with the march step of legionnaires, comes the time of the imperial religion of Love. One last time Cleopatra becomes the new incarnation of the goddess and holds against her breast the inimitable Anthony.

Aphrodite subdued, subsumed under Jesus Christ. Given over to infinite depths and heights. Given over to the sky and the ground, withdrawn from the sea on which he nevertheless walks.

Can we imagine in the midst of the foam the light step of a Son of man, a brother of Attis? But no, with him all the gods are gone. What arrives is a world of exiles, pilgrimages, great migrations and curiosities and worries. Stop all that coming and going: history is getting under way.

Aphrodite stops and returns to reign as the mother of God. Wise as an image, ready for the painting of love and flesh, the already aged, overblown troubles of a young culture. The Renaissance goes into mourning, into the widowhood of God. But Aphrodite is never more widow than virgin. Have we not understood? Or how are we to say?

‿〜

It is an old business, our most cherished tradition: the Greeks were *deeply superficial*; they conducted mourning with a serene smile. They never exposed or unbosomed themselves, or maybe for them exposing themselves was a way of covering up, hiding in a gracious nudity. Aphrodite is the sovereign of the Graces: the Khorites weave her cloak. Veil, skin, grain, reflections of the wine-dark sea, breasts, thighs, hair, a smile.

Aphrodite, the most Greek of Greeks and the least recognizable. She is archi-Hellenic, rather Semitic (**Attor(i)t* is the least improbable *etymon*). Trojan, Babylonian, Syrian, Ethiopian, Jew, Arab. Helen taken from Greece, returned to the East, lost in Egypt, given to the West. Mestiza Aphrodite.

Métis: nobody. *Mêtis*: wise and powerful prudence. Rome negotiating Greece and Carthage. Rome without race, unaccustomed to race, propagating everywhere the taste for embraces: *omnibus incutiens blandum per pectora amorem.*

There is no "race" there, especially not a race of gods.

The foam of peoples with the foam of their words, with the foam of the waves on their shores and under their oars. The foam of their days:

imagine seven thousand years of words and religions, navigations and hardships, between those andesite idols of uncertain sex and us, we who call up the foam of their names on the shining screen of a computer.

(Strabo's maps show twenty-six cities and places that carry the name Aphrodite, including Aphrodite Polis, the place where the sacred cow of Egypt is raised, not far from Crocodilopolis, and the place called Port Vendre—*Veneris Portus* in Latin.)

The foam of their nights: the goddess guiding their members, their couplings, laying them down on soapy rocks, putting her breasts, uncovered above her dress, into their hands—Aphrodite of the marvelous bosom, *perikallea deirē*, of the desirable chest, *stēthea imereuota*, "Milky Way, oh luminous sister/Of the white streams of Canaan," making the mixed liquids flow, mixing up languages, blood, narratives. Imagine the unimaginable night of time, depth without opacity rising toward us, *hominum divumque voluptas*.

᠅

(We are tired of this imagining. What sort of orgasms, what communions are you priding yourself on?

—You don't understand at all. I am only talking about obstinacy.

—And that's not derisory?

—Don't make me laugh.)

᠅

Today the myths are interrupted. They have not disappeared: for centuries, soon we can say for millennia, we have been playing in their foam. But the myth no longer speaks what it was supposed to speak (what it was supposed to speak, according to us): this word stated by the things themselves, by the atom, this offering of a nature, a world and an origin redeployed, turned into language and signs from out of themselves. Myth no longer speaks this founding word, and it should not speak it any more. A time has come when it is no longer possible for the origin to be spoken without becoming enraged and turning itself into the supplier of mass graves and charnel houses. Myth became the will of a race.

This is also why mourning happens without serenity, and stripping bare without a smile or a poem, and why there is destitution. A stiff foam, pornophilic aphrodisiac, and the obscenities of torture or starvation. And nothing or no one to give reason or to give thanks.

Myth no longer speaks the generative word, where sense is engendered out of itself, where the world curled up into itself, the language of its own sense, and the proper propriety of its language. If myth is interrupted, it simply means that this mode of sense is interrupted. The interruption of sense: this is, quite simply, the epoch known as "the West." Or indeed, the time that believes itself to be cut off from immemorial times.

Interrupted myth no longer speaks as it used to speak, mythically (as we think it used to speak: the Cypriot idols have never told us anything about what they used to say, if they said anything at all).

It is not that there is nothing left to say. It is not a matter of an apocalyptic silence. Out of the very place, or from behind the place where myth is interrupted, some word makes itself heard. This place is only the surface of the myth, the place where its depth of sense stops, the foam of Aphrodite.

Sense is no longer given, if it ever was. But the foam of words suggests sense. Something wet, streaming everywhere and running, slipping, evaporating. Sense that is always mixed up with other sense, with what is other than sense and with the sense of other things, *mestizo* sense. But the mixing of sense is not another myth. It is what we all are, the ordinary, unfigurable mélange, a figure that is so common and yet just as lost as a shapeless, seven-thousand-year-old idol. This mixing is not a substance; it does not form another depth. It is only the very slow movement of the mixing of men and men, men and gods, men and women. The saliva of confused words said lip to lip, faithfully.

Foaming sense, sing me.

࿊

Sing me the island fringed with foam, your land in the middle of the water. Goddess of Cyprus, where three towns are sacred to you. The island is not dry soil, nor an isolated place. It is bathed, its soil moistened on all sides. The foam gathers there, creating a surface, a skin—*chrōs*. *Amphi de leukos aphros ap'athanatou chrōs*. Skin that is not mortal and a detached piece, the arrival of the girl: *toi d'epi kourē ethrēphthē*. Skin and color, *chrōma*.

Aphrodite is an island. All the Islands are Aphrodite, but hers carries the name *Cyprus*. Chromatic Aphrodite is the color of copper, *Chyprios chalcos, cyprium aes, cuprum*. Only the metal of Cyprus contains cadmium, calamine, vitriol, and the ashy substance: this is according to Posidonius, and Strabo after him. The whole of the East, and Crete and Egypt too, came for copper. The Myceans came, and the Achaeans, Phoenicians, Assyrians, Persians. They came and mined, loaded up their vessels, occupied the towns, built forts, sanctuaries, and ports. The Greeks came and the Romans, Paul of Tarsus. The Byzantines came, the Arabs, Richard the Lionheart, the Knights Templar, and the Frankish Kingdom of Cyprus and Jerusalem. The Venetians came, Eudes of Montreuil, the Turks and the English. They came, left, and came back again.

Copper, bronzed Aphrodite, the color of sword and shield. War-Cyprus, sea from East to West, covered in the pillage, hatred, and wounds of all continents. The smile of the foam is now nowhere to be seen, not here and not on the other sea, the Gulf beyond the sands. A soldier sent there says: "When you're a kid you think it's fun. It's not."

᠈ᢩᡄ

(There is no longer any such thing as a paean of victory. The epic and all its singing have fallen silent. War without legends: it goes without saying.)

᠈ᢩᡄ

(What is left is the veiled voice.)

The depth that rises is birth. Foam is always nascent, only nascent. Aphrodite has no birth: she is birth, coming to the world, existence.

Birth needs foam. There has to be mixing and wetting for the thing itself to be born: its inimitable form. "The wet is the cause of the form taken by the dry," Aristotle says.

Empedocles gives a name to the place of birth: "the cleft lawn of Aphrodite." Goddess of gardens, *Aphrodite en kepois*. Sea of grass, sea grasses, seaweed, gulf weed, wrack, sea lettuce, lustrous hair, soaking fleece, birth of the cleft. What comes to the surface, what foams, is a cleft. The cleft is not a gash; it is a fork in the seaweed; it is a fruit, a fig half opened onto a damp froth. These are lips licked by the swell. To be born: the name of being. To be delivered, to come into the open of a place.

No gods: the luck of places.

And the sea, in the places where it is agitated, multiplies the laughter. Aeschylus called it *kumaton anarithmon gelasma*, the innumerable laughter of the billows. And much later Oppian of Cilicia called it *gelos*, the great sea with the gift of laughter, panther skin and torn cloak.

A cleft, an opening, but not an abyss or a gulf. It has no depth. *Hystera*, what is behind, deep down, comes to the fore. *Hysteron proteron* is a figure in rhetoric, also named hysterology. The speech of the goddess is a gentle, frothy hysteria with no anxiety, no power. A divinity with no force, *analkis theos*, but when she bleeds it is from here, *ichor*, that the immortal blood escapes, the blood whose flowing shines and is not an indication that something is dead.

Not even a step, nothing but the heaving up of water, a birth of the cleft that comes to the surface.

Paean to Aphrodite ■ *79*

Cyprus, the goddess of the island, gently lifts her cleft. She is, inconceivable, well conceived, the raising of a cleft, the mound of grass parted and her gem, her key, *kleitoris*.

~

Mastos, also, the breast: the birth of breasts. Once again, the *etymon* has to do with humidity. To be damp, to drip, to brim, to overflow. To be drunk. Outside sense, *aphrosune*. Cypriot drunkenness: literally exuberant existence. *Uber*, mammary, generosity, an *etymon* different from a breath, from that of the hyster (**ud-/udh*). Another smile on the wine-dark sea. And what a man envies in the breast of a woman, a swelling without arrogance, a peaceful rising up, abandon.

Breast, wave, fold. Wave, particle, light. This is the subject of the verb *to travel at the speed of light*. The breast is born like light, like dawn at the place where sea and sky fold into one another. Aphrodite, her eyes full of light, *ommata marmainonta*, golden Aphrodite, *chruse Aphrodite*.

The fold multiplies the occurrences of existence. The fold is not the fold of being: the fold is being itself.

Everything folds together at the tip of the breast. At every point, with every rising of the bottomless, anadyomene depths, everything folds, folds itself again and unfolds, the striations of sunken columns, the smooth grain of this stretch of skin, milky soul. The folds of the band that supports the breasts of the goddess, *poikilo*, embroidered with drawings in many colors, where everything is drawn from tenderness, love and *oaristys*. "Love": there is nothing mythical about it.

~

Aphrodite thinks: she weighs the weight of the foam. This vague, effervescent weight that weighs nothing on the deeps. *Argynnis aphrodite* is a brilliantly colored butterfly found in North America. The weight of a delicate flight that circumscribes no territory. That splits the seaweed and the waves, but leaves them mixed together, a foamy fleece, *aphrokomos*.

It is not a matter of being "so deep it's shallow." The dialectic breaks, like myth. The foam liquefies and liquidates it. Floating wood, teats and buds, shells washed by waves.

In all its differed, diffracted senses, only an expanse of sea, wide open under her arms, spilling out of the whiteness between her buttocks, in contact with the open sky.

This brightness is not blinding, but, at the same time, there is nothing about this naked birth of sense that offers guidance. No grammar, no logic, no faith, no politics. Thought must rise up naked.

Just as depth rises to the surface, the most ancient emerges as novelty, as what is to come. This lost flight of sense, which must have been the origin, comes back to us, just the same and completely changed: the panic of beginnings, the memory of our darkness, white with foam, set on the water, weighed, licked by the crests of the waves.

Strange Foreign Bodies

I

"Foreign body" is the name we use for any object, bit, piece or substance that is introduced in a more or less accidental way into an ensemble or a milieu that is otherwise organic or at least considered homogeneous and governed by its own regulations, rules to which the "foreign body" cannot be subjected. A concrete beam is a foreign body in a forest, a tin drum in a river. But the canonical example is still a needle or a bit of glass accidentally swallowed or, better yet, a surgical instrument forgotten after an operation and sewn up inside the body. In this last case, invasive intervention—as it is called in medical jargon—sees its therapeutic aim warped into aggression, all the more so since such carelessness sullies the image of the practitioner, his expertise and his duty. The forgotten "clamp" (this is the stereotypical example) becomes a foreign body twice over: foreign to the patient's body and foreign to the moral body of medicine. But the most exemplary case must surely be a different medical one: a malignant tumor. A visitor hostile to the organism that it undertakes to destroy by slow degrees, the cancerous cell has not yet revealed the exact secret of where it comes from. Does it come from the body itself or from elsewhere? Even when it seems clear that it comes from outside, the course of its development is not at all obvious. After all, not all smokers get lung or throat cancer.

The "foreign body" brings together the violence of an intrusion and the malignancy if not of an intention then at least of a disposition. This is thanks in part to the expression and in part to the imprecise image that it conjures up. But the intrusion is already the carrier of a potential malignancy. More broadly speaking, penetration itself is or could become suspect: it is difficult to speak of penetrating a body, a territory, or a thought without there being a air of menace or aggression about the words.

The notion that the stranger is threatening, or at least worrying, is an old one, as old as the idea of the stranger, which goes back at least as far as the first clan, the first group, even back before humanity itself, to all sorts of communal life, to given or elective affinities and thus to almost all sorts of life. After all, life is rarely lived without being shared and shared out in relationships, correlations, lines, partitions, and sharings.

The expression *foreign body* allows us to sense what the stranger consists in. It is not only a matter of its difference but also, and perhaps above all, the fact that this difference is the fact of a *body*—with this word taking on all its connotations of concrete resistance and autonomous hardness, fortified in a sufficiency that always shows itself, sooner or later, to be hostile to all other bodies. The word "body" [*corps*] resonates like "out" [*hors*] and "strong" [*fort*]: they are mentioned to indicate the force of real, physical exteriority, which can only be gauged in terms of material impenetrability. A body is penetrable only according to one of two opposing logics: the logic of assimilation or the logic of destruction. Either the foreign material is assimilated by the body—ingested, absorbed, metabolized—or it cuts into the integrity of the body, wounding it, tearing it, even mutilating or lacerating it. (If we talk about penetration without mentioning the threat of invasion—military or medical—we are talking about love. In the case of love, there is a mingling without either assimilation or laceration. There is one body in another, toward another without incorporation or decorporation. "Love" means the mingling of two that evades all the traps of the one.)

In the *foreign body*, body—in general—takes on all its connotations of exclusion: a body is what separates itself. A body is what relates to the outside only in terms of exteriority, distinction, isolation, no matter what sort of exchanges it can nonetheless find itself implicated in. When it shows itself as a *foreign body*, it is not in any relation that corresponds with its own properties. In this way it best reveals its naked property: the property of making body with itself.

A body makes body: this is not a tautology. It is a matter of attributing to a subject its essential attribute. If the soul is the form of the body (of an organized body, Aristotle says, though we must insist that the inorganic—the *res extensa*—is co-essential with the organic, since all body is first mineral, liquid, gassy, sinewy, etc.) then the body is also the impenetrability of the soul. It is the hardness, consistency, fortification of the soul. A soul with no fortifications, no ramparts, would faint away, inanimate.

II

Therefore, the body itself, the one we call "own," "my" body, is also a stranger. Every body is a stranger to other bodies: being a stranger is inherent in its corporeality. Above all, a body is extended, and this extension saves it from the unreal condition of the point. It cannot be said to be without dimensions. But its dimension, all its dimensions constitute so many instances of setting at a distance; other bodies have to move away. The distance between them opens up the condition of their relations: their contacts, confrontations, looks, listenings, tastes, and attractions.

My hands touch one another; my body recognizes itself coming to itself from an outside that it itself is, taking into itself again the world outside it. The chiasm of the flesh that is described so well by the most insightful phenomenology of the body—the chiasm that, thanks to an anagrammatical resonance between the French words *chair* ["flesh"] and *chiasme* ["chiasm"], allows us to sense how we are interwoven with the world—reminds us that our being entwined with the world has always, from the start, exposed us right down to our most intimate depths. The "inside" is always between outside and outside, and this *between*—the *between* of its lair, its cave of myths and phantoms of interiority—is, in the end, nothing but another *outside*. Distanced from all outsides though never arriving at a dimensionless point (because *the psyche is extended*: this time it is the analyst who claims to know), "inside" or "in itself" can only ever be given outside, an *internal outside* [hors interne] and not a *foro interno*.

The body does not contain anything: not a spirit, which could not ever be contained because it has no place or dimension or consistency, nor an interiority that would be the body's own interiority, since that itself would only be the multiply folded surface of the ex-position or ek-sistence that it *is*. This is what it means to say that the soul is the form of the body; it is the whole, entire surface exposed, with no front and back, no double face, no doubling, no lining, but from all sides exposed, like those topological entities that do not allow any opposition between inside out and right side out.

Right down to the depths of its viscera, between the fibers of its muscles and all along its irrigation channels, the body exposes itself, exposes to the outside the inside that constantly recedes, fleeing ever deeper into the depths of the abyss that it is. For this is the truth of the world. Issuing forth out of nothing, *created*, that is, not produced, not formed, not constructed, but the alteration and spasm of the *nihil*, the world is the explosion and expansion of an exposition (which we may call "truth" or "sense"). The chiasm of body and world exposes exposition to itself—and with it, the impossibility of finally bringing the world back to a spirit and sense to a signification. The world is a strangeness that is preceded by no familiarity.

III

Bodies are strangers: they are made of the outside, of the *extraneitas* that makes up the strangeness of the stranger. The outside always appears to come after the inside, as a milieu, an element in the midst of which the inside will have pre-existed, detached, gathered into itself. But this gathering, this enveloping on the inside can only take place by means of the detachment that develops the outside. This cannot be reduced to representing a "non-self." On the contrary, it forms the possibility of exposition without which the "self" itself could quite simply not be, that is, be in relation with itself. All the evidence points to outside and inside being the condition of one another, and the inside can be defined in only two ways: either as pure concentration in self—in which case it is called "spirit" or "mind"—or as relation to self, in which case it is called "soul." But spirit, a stranger to all dimension, extension, and form, has no outside. It is the all-encompassing absolute, self-enveloping in such a way that it suppresses in itself all distinction, right down to the distinction between the front and back of the envelope. Spirit is in this sense the absolute stranger, the foreignness to the world of a radical negation of all exteriority. *Extraneus extremus, interior intimo meo*—the stranger as equal to unfathomable intimacy, other as more same than the most same, sameness dissolved in identity, and identity collapsed into itself.

This is also why spirit—which runs everything through with its point, passes through all with its breath or flame and reverberates through itself above all, pure ignition, pure combustion, an exhalation that runs out of breath, the inspiration of an expiration, spirit that is equal only to death—is finally reduced, in the ultimate concentration and contraction that bind it, to the throbbing, bursting desire to get out of itself. This desire makes the soul possible.

Spirit surges forth in its desire for the outside; the soul responds by forming itself: body turned to the outside, exposing desire. This desire springs from nothing other than the absolute strangeness of spirit. In the world there is an extraneousness of the world. The sense of the world is outside the world, and this outside is itself outside the whole, deprived of place, outside without inside. This is why spirit—sense, sense as breath—leaps outside the absence of place, exploding the point that it is (its essential nullity), opening dimension, the spacing of forms, the distancing of bodies.

IV

Bodies are strangers to one another thanks to the foreignness [*étrangèreté*] of the spirit that animates them. This extraneousness constitutes their strangeness [*étrangeté*]. Not only are bodies strange, but they do not recognize one another and approach one another only with difficulty, obliged to overcome at least a certain mistrust, and sometimes a fear or even repulsion. A body does not easily touch another body, because it knows that this proximity threatens to strike them both down in a new flaring up of the desire of spirit.

In a certain way, all bodies touch. The world is woven from the contiguity of all the bodies between whom air, light, sound, scents, and all the other modulations of material constantly weave the fine, tightly woven cloth of the universe. The last owes its name to the unity of this cloth and nothing else, the unity of extension entwined with itself, unity that is not resolved in unification or uniformity, unity essentially distanced from itself and exposed to itself: bodies among themselves, sharing their *between*, their *with*, their *against*—against one another, close and intermingled without resolution. Nothing resolves the world into spirit: this is not a fault or a lack, quite the contrary, for the One is not the good that beings run the risk of missing or being separated from (all that impoverished logic and impoverished morality of mutilation, necessary castration, resignation to separate being). The One is itself lack, lack in itself par excellence; the One dissolves in solitude, deprived of everything, even position, deprived of unity and subsistence.

Nothing remains except distinct bodies and the indefinite variation, constantly replayed, of their distinctness. Souls turned to one another, to touch one another, side by side or face to face, back to back and each in turn. Forms that brush against one another and avoid one another, that conform to one another or deform one another, fold one another, marry one another, and break up. They never melt into one another or become confounded, although they sometimes disappear, taking the form of molecules or colors, always reanimating distinct contours, separating or dilating marks and traces, borders, fringes, trembling extremities on which bodies reach the high point of their exposition: dandruff, thin skin, narrowings or broadenings, birthmarks and other such distinctions, the fading away of substances.

Leaf against leaf and grain among grains, streams of water divided by a few mounds of earth, twins born of a single divided egg, masses of rock and the flights of vultures, right hand and left hand, smoke reflected on the lake, the lantern fish in the great depths of the ocean, the worn-out back of the rice picker, and you, and you again, or me, you who say "me" and I who say "you," and our lips thick or thin, and the contrasting composition of our faces, constantly challenging any attribution of individual essences. Further, in a still more singular way, the strangeness from one moment to another of a supposed subject, callouses and wrinkles, scars, varicose veins, stains, vanishing lines.

V

Singular essences are mobile, volatile, always different from themselves and always deferring their essentialness—without, for all that, giving up on the promise of a sameness, a final propriety that would have all the force of an Idea: this stone, this fern, this woman.

This Idea owes its force to the constant reaffirmation of its necessity according to spirit—but, as we have already said, spirit does not show off its desire for the outside: that this stone, this fern, this woman should come to be only by emerging from itself, offered to the winds, to fire, to encounters. In this exposition, a body is not only a stranger to others. It is such by also being a stranger to itself. A body alienates itself, estranges itself. It is the foreignness and strangeness to self of a soul thrust out, ejected from the non-place of the spirit.

A body is the withdrawal from self that relates a self to itself as it exposes the world. My body is not just my skin turned toward the outside: it is already itself my outside, the outside in me and for me—opposed by me to myself in order to distinguish me from unity. A stranger to others and first of all to this other that I become thanks to it. Where am I? In my foot, my hand, my genitals, my ear? Where am I in this face, these traits, traces, eccentricities, tremblings? Who am I on the contours of this mouth that says "I"?

Own body—this is what we say to distinguish it from the foreign body: but owned by virtue of what ownership? Proper according to which propriety? It is not an attribute of my substance; it is not a possession I have by right, even if I can in certain respects identify it as filling one of these roles. It is proper insofar as it is me rather than insofar as it is mine. If it was mine like an attribute or a possession, I could abuse it to the point of destroying it. Me destroying myself only shows that it is me and not mine.

It is indeed me, myself, *ego extraneus*. Myself on the outside, myself outside as outside me, myself as the division between an inside and an outside, the inside sunken down into itself to the obscure, opaque, abysmal point of concentration where spirit tears itself in two: into an abstract "I" that "must accompany all my representations," as Kant would have it, the logico-grammatical subject deprived of any consistency, and an uttered "I," a wide-open *ego* on two lips that round themselves around a column of air that is made to resonate by my throat, palate, and tongue according to the frequencies required by the particular physique of my language. The inside is thereby turned on itself, extravasculated, exogastrulated, exclaimed, expressed and thrown—not "outside" but "as the outside."

Yes, me-outside. Not "outside me" because in truth the only inside is not "me" but the gaping in which a whole body gathers and pulls itself together in order to find a voice and announce itself as "self," reclaim itself and call itself, desire itself in desiring the echo that will perhaps come back from the other bodies around it. Stranger to itself in its call from itself: otherwise, it would not be called at all, it would not express with all its extension the demand to meet this stranger.

VI

Making body, it estranges itself—it, the point of spirit. It takes form, takes on soul, becomes animated, made strange to itself. Better still, what animates it is this foreignness, this strangeness that comes to it from the depths of its abyss. Without it, it would remain without soul, pure spirit shattered into pieces of bone, fiber, humors, sweat . . .

Body in a rising and falling tide, flux and reflux, flow and ebb, the sea heaved up, welling up from a depth that is before all life, before the first cellular division of this very body, before the whole multiplication of bodies starting from the thick, dense *nihil*.

The strange that occupies it and urges it on holds out its palms and lips, its forehead, its pupils, the rise and fall of all its limbs and members, its constraints and comforts, its ways, its shocks of hair, its edges, ridges, angles, nails. It advances and offers itself, ventures in the direction of lights and smells, towards speckles, roughnesses, stabilities, and softnesses; it braves shrillness and growls, blows and vibrations. It incorporates into itself this cavernous body occupied by shadows, and becomes the scent of a rose or the wool of a carpet, the grating of chalk, the streaming flow of clouds or lava. It then withdraws and sheds its skin, an immaterial sketch whose waters cradle a reflection. It returns to the sea and the sand, uncertain of its own contours, which have been expanded by effort or by boredom, slipping outside itself like a dead skin.

Becoming stranger and stranger to itself, tattooed by age and passion, pleated and stained by the movements of its tastes, distastes, impulses and refusals—this whole machinery of attraction and retreat that exposes it, one galaxy among galaxies, to the explosion or implosion of forces that puts it together and sets it in motion—it finally recognizes itself for what it is: the visitor who has come from way back, the reptile and rodent, the bird, the insect grafted onto the embryo, a bundle of nerves that suddenly emerges with a jolt out of nothingness.

It is itself its jolt, its spasm. It is nothing but one more shudder in an embrace between two bodies, becoming the body of the *between* opening a new space, a new outside from it to the others and first of all from it to itself, just one more distancing, one more estrangement between all bodies, all of them strangers thrown into the world and at themselves, the feverish multitude and the gleam of our dust.

VII

The swimming body is a fin, a fish's tail and the glistening scale; it becomes a current and a liquid mass, seaweed and a pale, sea-green brightness. The eating body becomes taste and gravy, the chewing of fibers and spices, pressed juice, expanded taste. The coming body is aggravated in the throes of its spasm, becomes transformed into a hardened trembling, and ends up dripping and ruptured. Each time, body is other and another than the one it is in all its avatars, all the divine metamorphoses in which it visits itself, angel or demon come from some distant elsewhere. Body came into itself from the unknown, the irruption and intrusion of other bodies, ingestions, intussusceptions, incarnations, recognitions and gratitudes, repulsions and rejections. Body is the great battering of foreign bodies, inspired and expired, gasping for breath, swallowed down and spat out.

It is a stretched strap and a relaxed fist, the hidden mass of sleep, palm to forehead, the echo of his voice in his head, vertigo, magnanimity and perspiration, the meanest excoriation, hardenings and cramps, irritations, obstructions, extrasystoles, sneezes, a whole machinery that is too sensitive, too susceptible to what is only the ever-renewed excess of all things—

and of itself—beyond the simple maintenance of its machine. For there is no machine; there is only desire and expectation, fear and hunger, need, want, impulse, and despondency. There is only the terrible struggle between forces that constrict one another, that pull and push on all sides, from all the extremities of the skin and of the world.

Body is itself in all its integrity only when it is dissected, anatomized, not when it is animated, frequented, inspired, knocked down, turned around, caressed. In this way it is thought, desire, impulse, virtue, inclination, and disinclination. It is east and west, zenith and nadir, sharing and crossing, regions of air, in the end a stranger to the world whose secret it carries—each body folded back, deployed as the secret of the world.

VIII

Body is nothing other than the strangeness of being. But body is only the body of the desire that reaches toward it—without that it is just a local contraction of forces. But its form quickly escapes it. The form of a body, this form that it is, corresponds to a desire, an expectation, even a need or a want: the form of the fruit I want to eat, of the hand I hope to hold.

The strangeness of being is due to this desire. Nothing is except thanks to the desire that it be. This desire comes from nowhere, or from *being* itself. Better still, it comes from *being*, it is of *being* and it is *being*.

Sense of the being, sense of being: to desire to be, to be the desire to be. The stranger, therefore, since desire makes itself strange to itself. *Ontology* and creation were the classical terms for this. We say them differently now, albeit in a parallel way, with our foreign bodies.

IX

We have always said it, and we will say it again now in still another way: the desire to be also bears the name "art." This belated, modern name designates in the singular the identity—which is in fact quite unsituateable—of a collection of practices and/or dispositions that used to be known as "fine arts" [or, translated literally, "beautiful arts," *beaux-arts*], a name in which strangeness is put into play twice over. On the one hand, "beautiful" [*beau*] designates nothing other than the quality of being strange to the whole order of causes and ends, reasons and intentions, functions and operations, organisms and mechanisms. "Beautiful" always names the disturbance of what is given, the intrusion of an excess, discomfort, nonconformity, and also whatever has to do with harmony, precision, and the happiness of touch. On the other hand, the "arts" designate no more than a technical operation (*technē, ars, Kunst* are the ways in which three different languages vary the motif of that capacity for extricating oneself from a problem, resolving a difficulty, a challenge that arises from the absence of a given means, an available function, a written program. These [various] techniques correspond to ends that are foreign to the ends we call the ends of "nature." This is how Aristotle can say that "art imitates nature." It substitutes itself for nature in order to do what nature does when nature does nothing.

Nature does nothing in order to respond to the desire to be. It is by definition the order of being without desire, of being that does not relate to itself as to a strangeness.

It would, of course, be only fair to be more specific and claim that the whole of being, and being as such, relates to itself as a strangeness. Without this it will be impossible to understand how "nature" can produce so very many superfluous forms and can have so many inexplicable ends—not least the end or purpose of the universe—or, indeed, how nature can produce in the higher mammals, on the one hand, a growing inferiority when it comes to spontaneous solutions and instinctive resources and, on the other, a growing complex of improbable ends, fragility, and destitution. The human animal is the extreme example of this. But if it is true that "nature" retains in itself a power of denaturation, this means that it has been alienating itself or becoming strange to itself from the moment of its own mysterious coming to be.

Denaturation is the principle of technologies—and thus the principle that means that there cannot be "technology" in the way that we say that there is "nature." There cannot be a unified technology that would give to being the means of its very being. Technology is by definition multiple and impossible to complete. It always multiplies its ends, which are in turn the means to ever-retreating ends, replayed and multiplied again.

Some technologies take on the task of denaturation as such and with that comes the dissemination of ends and the endless strangeness of the desire to be. This desire is indeed strange, because it desires nothing, no object, and it is foreign because it only desires what it has no sort of knowledge, representation, or anticipation of, only the thought that it desires, when all is said and done, to desire, which amounts to saying that it desires its own strangeness.

We call these technologies the "arts." They consist in giving form and value to this strangeness of desire and this desire for the stranger. A man puts his hand on a rock wall and blows a colored powder around it; he takes his hand away and contemplates the clear imprint outlined by the dusting of ochre or carbon. Or he lifts up his foot and taps the ground in such a way as not to set his body off in the motion of walking but to give it the impulse of being suspended over the ground, to twist and bend for its own sake, like a hanging vine or a cloud. This dance and this image carry in themselves all the strangeness of a body that knows itself, or surprises itself, a stranger to itself.

Still, it is not that "art" domesticates and thereby reduces the strangeness of this body. On the contrary, it exposes it and deepens or accentuates it, exaggerates it if need be, aggravates it, tracks it down only in order to let it escape. It opens for it the space of limitless expansion.

The Body of Pleasure

I

What is a body of pleasure? It is a body detached from the schemas of perception and operation. It is no longer available to sight, or to sensation in general, in any of the usual ways of its functional, active, relational life. It is not turned toward the world, not even toward the other with whom—since we're talking about sexual pleasure—it is engaged in an exchange. There is no longer an "other" in the ordinary sense of the word, just as there is no self-sameness or fusion. The two (maybe more) are caught up in a mingling that is not just a mingling of these different bodies but at the same time the blurring of all the distinctions, roles, or operations connected to the functions, actions and representations of daily life—indeed, of life whether daily or not. Think, for example, of a sportsman in the field, an actor on stage, or anyone engaged in intense work. In any case, what is blurred is everything that is organized for—subordinated to—the task of effecting something external.

In contrast, the body of pleasure is organized only according to itself. The same holds for the suffering body, though in the mode of refusal, resistance, and repulsion, whereas pleasure is appealing and is requested again and again indefinitely. What is refused in one case and claimed in the other is the same thing: a body recomposed (or decomposed or compounded) according to a composition that is unlike all those compositions in which its actions can be effective. It is a body mingled with itself and organized by this mingling. It is mingled with itself and with another (or others), with self *as* other. It becomes a stranger to itself in order to relate to itself as another or even itself as the other who encroaches upon it and besieges it, in order to enjoy it [*jouir de lui*] and also rejoice in itself [*ré-jouir lui-même*].

Thus the body of pleasure is for itself only insofar as it abandons the order of self-preservation, the maintenance of vital functions and techno-logical aptitudes, and does so with a certain autofinality. What is pre-served here (if we want to use Spinoza's term) or what affirms itself is the body as a capacity for transforming itself, reforming itself, or, perhaps, informing or even *exforming* itself, passing from conformation, even con-formity regulated by a collection of social, cultural, and technological practices, to a form that is itself always in the process of formation.

This body invents itself, recomposes and replays itself. It re-forms itself and almost ex-forms itself, indeed de-forms itself in such a way that it is now nothing more than this exposition of self; body as skin touched and touching, that is to say, as the modulation of an approach that always begins again from the proper limit of body. It reaches its limit, it passes its limit, it makes itself limitless.

The body of pleasure tends toward limitlessness, as if it were no longer body at all but pure soul. In the same way, the opposite movement, pain, tends to reduce the suffering body to a suffering soul that concentrates itself in the burning and its rejection of it or, more precisely, in this burn-ing such that it rejects itself. Pleasure and pain are like two modes of being burned: a burning that feeds on itself and one that resists and repulses itself.

These are two modes of excitation: excitation is the movement of ap-peal by and response to an exterior agent. Excitability is an elementary property of living beings. The living are above all excited, called upon to respond to an outside. As a result, the living being is always already re-sponding to this call, always already excited, affected by an outside. In-deed, it is being affected by an outside that brings anything to life, whether we are talking about a plant or a human animal. (This is how to understand the representation of the world as a big animal: the world is the living thing excited by the empty outside of a non-world that it names *nothing* or *god*, two equivalent ways of talking about this first touch.)

In pleasure and pain, excitation is taken for itself; that is to say, the outside in this case is at least comparable to the *nothing-god* of the outside of the world. Excitation does not refer to and is not directed toward the outside of the rest of the world when it is a matter of perceiving, receiving or communicating, acting, and so on. But the outside is the body itself, or nothing, or another body as the *again* of indefinite contact with the totality of bodies, of the world; contact across this refers, in a deeper way, to the furthest limits of the world, its creation and its end.

To think this we must free pleasure and pain from their finalized interpretations: here, pleasure is not the delight that indicates something useful or salutary and pain is not just a way of making us aware of a nuisance. We must bring to bear, without hesitation, the determination of pleasure as a *demand*: call, incitation, excitation to go beyond utility and satisfaction in order to go toward the dismantling of self, abandon, to pass to the limit—a passage that does not clear a way but that brushes past, touching as it goes and in touching lets itself be touched by the outside (nothing-god).

Every way of talking about "jouissance" that falls under the legal sense of complete possession and therefore repletion or satis-faction, an "enough" with which a "self" would be "contented," remains trapped in a confusion between jouissance or joy and this contentment that we have just named. To be content is also to "content oneself with." It falls within the realm of what is useful and reasonable. But pleasure does not content itself. This may even be why it confines itself to discontent, while jouissance undoes itself in the excessiveness of its own excitation. But within these confines, where pleasure and pain are located side by side, lies exactly the area where the game of the limit is played out: insurmountable but touched, as surpassed touch, but as touching, pushing inside what cannot get out because this outside does not exist (it is not another inside).

There is no outside, and this is how it is outside, how it puts me outside myself: this is the experience of pleasure. In this sense we could say that pleasure is always the infinite approach of pleasure, but this cannot be understood in terms of deception and privation. Certainly it is legitimate to talk of "finitude" and to say that pleasure is finite. It is essentially finite because it reaches the end, the limit where the body tends to lose all form, becomes matter, an impenetrable mass. But this *end* also forms the touch of the outside and with it the joy of the world.

II

The body mingled with itself and with an other (or others), with itself *as* with the other, does not enter into identification or confusion, but rather into a proximity that is troubling because pleasure consists in tasting the always uncertain, unstable, and trembling measure of proximity, the approach of a certain distinction and renewal, repetition and revival of distance.

To touch: that is, to set in play both attraction and repulsion, integrity and breaking apart, distinction and translation. To set in play *together* as such, that is, the light touch of unity and its abandonment, its disunion.

The touched and touching body—touched because it touches, touching because it is touched, always having elsewhere the sufficient reason of its bodily being—this body organizes itself around itself, that is, around this contact of bodies that has no end other than itself, around this contact that is also the contact of the same body with itself. For it is precisely in this way that it no longer is or has a "self" but is exposed in its entirety. It exposes itself first by posing itself outside the order of needs, functions, services, or offices. Its office becomes the service of pleasure, which means the service of the movement by which a body recalls itself, gathers itself, and revives itself for itself, to set itself in resonance with the outside of bodies.

This body emerges from its form. Its heart no longer beats to the rhythm of a blood pump but instead to the rhythm of wild panic; its lungs no longer respire but pant, even suffocate in the attempt to draw a breath that would be the suspension of breath itself and the cutting off of air. Its limbs and organs are no longer limbs and organs but are deformed and reform in zones, parcels, or disoriented continents whose entire geography expands or contracts according to the excitations that at every point raise the possibility of a complete recomposition. A body that would arise completely from a breast, a palm, a belly.

Among these various zones, the ones that distinguish and assert themselves are those that are the sites of an effusion, a spurt, a flowing of humor, liquor, that is, a solution/dissolution of form in which an incessantly new possibility of form is sketched.

Everything is there, in the sketch of an indeterminate recomposition out of which another body would spring, another sharing of bodies, another mingling and unmingling of skins, a *liquidation* of organic and social contours and constructions.

In sex, bodies testify to a vocation for infinitizing oneself beyond all secondary determinations of a given order. This is why sex is the place of creation: of making children or forming forms, assemblages and configurations, rhythms and resonances. Starting from nothing, that is, opening wide what is already itself only opening: mouth, eye, ear, nostril, sex, anus, skin, skin indefinitely reclaimed and all its pores reopened. Spacings, generosities, captures and abandonments, comings and goings, swings: always the syncopated cadence of an gait that carries toward the confines of what is delimited, by a body first of all.

The body of pleasure (and its reverse, the body of pain) illimits the body. It is its transcendence.

There Is Sexual Relation—and Then

I

First of all, I chose this title simply because what I wanted to do there—in Mireille Calle-Gruber's seminar—was to pursue a bit further the reading of a small piece I had devoted a few years earlier to the Lacanian axiom: "There is no sexual relation." What you have before you is an approximate transcription of what I presented at the seminar. The presentation itself was based only on a few notes because the object of the meeting was above all to talk with the students and to engage with a presentation made by Eberhardt Grüber.

Of course, I would hope that "and then" would also open up the possibility of a more ample development of the perspectives sketched out. We have by no means finished with the question of "relation" in general, and everything that the Lacanian axiom seems to have helped close over as much as open up must be brought back into play in every possible way. After all, our thinking remains preoccupied with the "subject," "gender," and even "plurality" and "singularity," and in this context *relation* is the term on which most work still needs to be done.

I will add still another possible use of this "and then," something that occurred to me after the seminar, after presenting these notes. You will already have heard the phrase in the form of a question—"and then?"—and in the tone of querulous defiance that goes along with this way of putting it. So what? What's it to us? What do we want with it? For this is indeed the question: What does it want with us, this relation that, after all, we could do without, and that, as is becoming ever more apparent, is not necessarily linked to the reproduction of the species, which can now be guaranteed in other ways.

In other words, after the sexual relation has generated a child, what is left? There is still the relation. It is a question of the repetition of the sexual relation for itself—for pleasure! (Do we know what that means? This is indeed the question.) And this question belongs to its very essence. "And then" is therefore always also "after the relation, then comes another one."

But it is also a matter of this question: "After the relation, and before the other, what [is there] of the relation?" Nothing, as we know. A form of sadness, a certain despondency, that is, the lying low that for a little or a long while separates, on the one hand, a brief exhaustion, a "satiation" (an "enough!" that is a no-longer-being-able-to-go-any-further that itself is infinitely divided between plenitude and emptiness), and, on the other, the beginning again of relation, that is, of desire, of its signs and motions and emotions.

II

I recall now the very simple assertion I made in that essay: Lacan's axiom uses the resources provided by the double meaning of the word *rapport* (like the word *relation*); *rapport-bilan* (*report* in English) and relation understood as an activity that goes from one to the other, or, rather, the act of between-two that is neither the one nor the other (neither of the two, nor their presumed unity, nor their simply disjunctive duality). There is no report, no account to be given, no result or product or accomplishment—*achievement* in English—of the sexual relation, and it is precisely according to this measure that there is, indeed, "sexual relation."

The fact that *rapport*, in its primary sense in French (the active sense "I have no rapport with this person") is not reducible to a state, a substance, or a term is not a philosophical (or mathematical) discovery. There is a long history to be written of the epistemological and ontological thought of *rapport*.

Relation [*rapport*] is neither being nor becoming. Of course there has to be some sort of relation for a being—whatever it is—to become, but the relation itself is neither the being nor its becoming. Relation withdraws from these categories, unless, of course, it is the other way around, and it makes more sense to think of relation coming first (quite simply:

first the group, parents, then the child . . .; first language, then the subject; first differentiation, then gender or sexual inclination).

"In the beginning is relation." This will have to be the formula, if the "is" here is not a contradiction. But it is certain that being, understood in the ordinary way (substance, subject, stance, boundaries) cannot be at the beginning, for how could it emerge from itself? This is the principle of thought from Plato to Hegel to us . . .

Being—always in this sense, let us call it the sense of classical ontology, which, to keep it simple, is distinct from ontology as Heidegger practiced it after Hegel and then passed it on to Deleuze and Derrida—must, on the contrary, appear as what we get to by subtracting from relation. Someone, someone withdrawn from all his relations—what is left of him? This is another question, one I will leave wide open, open in principle to the response: he remains "one," always indefinitely withdrawing further away.

III

Let us remember that "one = nothing," nothing that has any sort of stability or solidity. "One" consists in withdrawing from itself, if every self implies being caught up in some relation that differentiates it both from others and in it-self (in order for it to be "it/self"). Relation designates what goes from "one-nothing" to or toward another "one-nothing." It is what goes from one term, whose position withdraws indefinitely, to the other, which also withdraws. But it is not as if there is a "this" that "goes." There is no mobile subject of this mobility. There is a proximity: a *with* that is other, that is to say, "beside" (*apud hoc*).

Here, proximity is the major category, proximity or intimacy, and, in general, it is a matter of superlatives: the closest, innermost, what penetrates most deeply into these areas, into these nooks and crannies, into the secret (the sacred?) of the "one" as well as the other. What is important is that the superlative of the reabsorption of distance is no more than an extreme intensification, not an annulment. What does *extreme* mean in general? A limit reached but not abolished. Reaching the limit is what relation is all about. (This is also what touching as such is all about, and the sexual relation is the epiphany of touch: of the kiss, of "fucking.")

The real category is not exactly proximity but approach. It is not a matter of a state but rather a movement (a quite local movement, as well as a variation of intensity and the transformation of a state). Approach has two essential characteristics: on the one hand, it is interminable (for the terms are fleeting, asymptotic) and, on the other hand (and as a result), it takes place in zones, that is to say, in a way that is discontinuous, fragmentary, part of the logic of a non-unity. In the end, this means that approach carries within itself both advance and recoil, taking up the approach again and again. (Not only, therefore, in the rhythm of a sexual act, a rhythmic logic of the caress, of friction, of intensifying repetition, but also that of the beginning again of acts, without any definable program.)

IV

An approach presupposes relation to a zone, to a determinate location (which is nevertheless not entirely determined, since all of the skin can become a "zone," as Freud pointed out), and it has the body multiply its own unity. It becomes both "here" and "there." I leave aside the question of the specification of those zones that, despite everything, are more marked sexually, and the character of this marking—orality, anality, genitality. Here I am considering just the fact that these more determined zones are revealed only in the context of a zoning of the whole ensemble, and in the general approach that assumes a discontinuous body, that is, a body distinguished from its unitary schema.)

The repetition of the approach means that the "one"—unlocatable or always withdrawn into the locale, the zone, the detail—is always a matter of coming and going. This is the same as the movement of the painter, the photographer, maybe also the musician and the artist generally speaking: the approach of a unity that is nothing but the fact of its parts or details (to the point where it is doubtful whether one is right to say "its" details). What is it that makes an image art? The back and forth between the details and the whole.

The practice of this approach is called attention. Attention, tension and inclination toward, choosing and valuing according to preference, cherishing the zone, the detail (think of Cèzanne with his "little perceptions," or of Wittgenstein asking that "this blue here" be reproduced for him, or of micro-tonal music, etc.). Attention differs from phenomenological intentionality in that it is not orientation toward an object but rather intensity brought to bear on (or toward, or right at, in contact with) a locality with which it is not confused but with which it becomes place, in contiguity and contagion. This "taking place" is called "pleasure" because it gives access to unity in the zone, leaving behind a presumed or assumed unity (integrated, perceptive, organized) in favor of an explosive unity, that is to say, a unity that is explosive and brilliant.

(Generally, we set all instances of *ad*—attention, adhesion, addiction, adoration, aversion—in opposition to those of *in*- (intention, invasion, intrusion, inspection, incorporation . . .) But the *ad-* is not for all that the contradiction of the *in-*: it forms the ex-position of the in-ternal or the in-timate in the sense that this last does not exist in itself as in a unity.

V

If the absolute incommensurability of relation in general is set up in this way—relation as not commensurable with the "one" in any way that would make it one of two or one among several or even the unity of these two or several, and also relation as not offering a self-commensurate unity—then it could be said that sexual relation represents the incommensurability of relation on its own terms—isolated and played out for itself. The sexual relation is the playing out of relation *kat'exochēn*.

It could be said, then, that, in a certain regard, all relations can be perfected, accomplished, saturated, and/or exhausted (a connection is made, an exchange, a meeting, a sharing, an association . . .) but that the sexual relation represents the unaccomplishment of relation. Or, put a better way, it could be said that *the sexual in all relation* (linguistic, social, affective, aesthetic) resides in the dimension of unaccomplishment. There is sex where there is no production, no result, and no positing of any sort of term.

Sex as a bodily determination—"sexuality" or "sexuation"—is the setting into relation of the body. The body is itself, in a general way, a setting into relation; it is always already in relation insofar as it is essentially ex-position (*ex-peausition*, as I have suggested elsewhere), extraversion, e-vasion. Sex is the determination of ex-position for its own sake and with no other end (therefore endlessly, absolutely).

This is not to say that "sex" is determined. Quite the contrary. It leaves quite open the consideration of different sexes and the way in which it is possible to distribute them—or not—to impute them—or not—and to implicate or disimplicate them in the matter of "identities" that are as biological as they are ontological, sociological, or otherwise. The distribution of sexes in the midst of all the instability and plasticity that there can be between and within us is of little importance here. The only thing that counts is the general disposition of *sexion*. This is a pseudo-term that I am using in passing, not in order to evoke sectioning, that is, splitting or division into parts (especially since the etymology does not support this occasionally attempted approach, leaving the word *sexus* without clear provenance), but in order, rather, to indicate something like a *self-ex-posing*, or a *self-ex-porting* outside oneself before even being constituted as "self," and therefore a being ex-posed and a being in relation that precedes and opens in advance all possible "being" and "becoming." It is a matter of a transcendental, a condition for the possibility of being as being to, or even an existential in the sense used by Heidegger (who does not understand sex as one such existential; see Derrida's analyses for more on this subject).

If we still must find some element of sectioning in sex (the paradigm is the sectioning of being one that is found in Aristophanes' speech in the *Symposium*), it would have to be in such a way that the One to whom sectioning happens never takes place; sectioning will always have preceded it. It is therefore no longer sectioning, no longer division or separation from anything whatever. It is originary relation, originary exposition, and this should be understood as the exposition of the origin itself. If the origin "is" relation, then the origin is dispersed into relation.

VI

The sexual relation is the fact that we have no origin and no way of being the origins of ourselves. Relation is the archi-originary frenzy of self-constitution, self-engendering. This holds for all relations, and the relations of relations that together weave our existences—but the sexual is responsible for making evident and presenting the "this" itself.

This is why it divides itself in two: on the one hand, into the possibility of engendering another (which would be a "result" or a third term only in a fleeting sort of way, entering, in its turn, into sexed self-sectioning) and, on the other, the possibility of relation without relation, which is what we have been talking about since the beginning.

No result, no accounting, no reason given, and besides, no question posed: no end, in any sense of the word. No question, but an address, an appeal—sex appeal.[1] An appeal that demands nothing but to be understood. It does not even really want a response, just to be thrown back again by the other in such a way that the relation takes place, back and forth, approach and repetition.

In Clarence Brown's film *Come Live with Me*, the man has told the woman about fireflies, who light up in order to spark the sexual instinct in their fellow fireflies. Later, the woman returns to her room, which is separated from the man's room in such a way that a ray of light can shine through the space above a partition and into where he is. She uses an flashlight—given to her earlier by the man because there was no light in her room—to send a signal to him, to signal her desire. This blinking light is not treated just as a signal. Here, between the reference to fireflies and the end of the film—which comes without showing us any sexual relation—it becomes a sign with no signification beyond itself, not only the sign of a *self-exposure* but a sign that is itself entirely formed by its own exposition, its light, its brilliance, with a magnificent flash that sheds light on nothing and that only trembles, trembles like a spasm. Self like a luminous spasm in the night of relation.

I've spoken of desire: it is not a question of desire for an object. It is not relation to something; it is relation to (tension toward, at-tention to) nothing but the relation itself.

VII

This is why we can add here a reflection on the language of sexual relation, or language in sexual relation. When we speak in love (since this is also how we designate this act, a fact that surely requires more attention), it is not in order to say anything other than the relation itself (its desire, its pleasure). This tautology, which I propose to call the erotic exclamation, has the remarkable characteristic of being one of the occasions (along with poetry and maybe also phatic utterances) where language is used in a way that carries it to the limit of significance. The formula is the exclamation repeated by de Sade: "I'm coming!" [*Je jouis!*]. This is the linguistic redundancy of sex, or indeed a sexual redundancy of language, which moves these two major modes of relation toward one another. But it is not as if the one ever stopped approaching the another—without ever becoming confused with the other, but also never ceasing to refer to it as its condition or its most distant and most secret issue. We speak in order to come, and we come in order to speak—which is also to say that each one, both sex and language, substitutes for the other, and also excludes the other, exhausts and excites the other;

"I'm coming!"—but also "You're coming!" and also "Come!" (Blanchot and Derrida, the "come" of a coming without end)—says nothing, but it utters (brings out, exposes) the "there is" of the sexual relation, of this relation that there is in effect each time precisely where there is nothing to say about it, nothing to report.[2]

And then—we say nothing, we begin again, we come again.

Appendix: Exclamations

Introductory note: This piece does not really have the encyclopedic character of a dictionary article in the sense that its object is not available in advance and not susceptible to treatment as one of the givens of the general field to which this volume is devoted. It is, rather, an object in the process of construction, as is clear from the sheer difficulty of choosing a title for the entry, a difficulty that continues, insofar as only the context of this dictionary can suggest the precise sense we want to give the term *exclamations* here. It is a matter of considering the pornographic signification or use of the use of speech in the sexual relation. (Moreover, the word is used in certain general descriptions, such as: "orgasm may be accompanied by exclamations or shuddering." But there is no term that can be regarded as proper to the signification under consideration here, not even a pregnant term, as is the case with the word *position*. In the midst of several possible reasons, we can point out the fact that we are dealing here with a very broad range, which can include whole sentences, indeed whole discourses, as well as interjections, cries, groans: we are in an indeterminate, variable zone situated at the limit of language.)

ॐ

"Oh heaven, if Lucifer himself were in the throes of unloading there wouldn't be this much froth, and the blasphemies and imprecations he would fling at the gods wouldn't be as appalling as this."[3] This comparison serves to characterize the behavior of one of de Sade's characters.[4] As we know, in de Sade as in many other places in erotic literature, exclamations accompany the sex act, and particularly its supreme moment. The same is true of cinema—porn or not—and even some songs (e.g., "Je vais et je viens," by Serge Gainsboug, or even "Que je t'aime," by Johnny Hallyday). The range of words used in this way, and the tones in which they are uttered, can vary from a cry or a belch to a murmur or a grunt, as between two limits where language fades away. Thus the obscene and blasphemous utterances of the Sadian hero could be replaced by the series of *Please*s and *yes*es we find in a very delicate scene in *Everything Is Illuminated*, by Jonathan Safran Foer.[5] We could also think of the religious expression *ejaculation*, which means a very short, private prayer repeated fervently, an expression whose accidental obscene connotation has often caused a smile. The ejaculatory prayer is at the heart of the Hesychast tradition, whose name means a quietness achieved by the fervent repetition of an exclamation.

It is surely not by accident that the name of a film—*Cries and Whispers*—takes in both extremities of the whole broad range of exclamatory or exclamative possibilities. Even though the name of the film was not chosen with any intent of referring to what concerns us here, it is still often taken up in pornographic places and sites.

Even if the distance between the two possible extremes is absolute, and even if these extremes oppose one another like the peak of cruel jouissance on one side and the peak of amorous joy on the other, a thin, almost imperceptible thread runs through the whole range of exclamation (even if, moreover, this is the fact and the expression—in Greek—of an *erastes* in the throes of possessing or an *eromenos* at the climax of being possessed) that can be organized according to the various possible combinations of the four elementary declarations: " I'm fucking you/I'm coming/ you're fucking me/you're coming." This continuous thread corresponds to what we can call a fundamentally pornographic characteristic, even if it is some-times pornographic only in a virtual or tendential way: there is something latent and asymptotic that is at least possibly pornographic about the very fact of utterance in the act of love. This is the reason for this dictionary entry. If pornography is defined as an exposition of the inexposable, not only in the sense of indecency but also literally in the sense of what cannot be shown, for example, the emission of sexual fluid, whether feminine or masculine, and the emotion of coming, experiencing jouissance (every-thing turns here on these two notions: emission and emotion), then we understand how exclamations, whether their meaning is directly sexual or rather more amorous ("I love you" *also* falls within the range evoked: everything depends on the tone) are, in themselves, already in lived reality an inchoate form of pornography, which is why pornography properly speaking must make use of them. Here speech comes to show what can-not be shown, or comes to underline that there is an excess beyond what is showable—like a paradoxical excess of meaning above and beyond sen-suality itself and like a supplement of avowals of the unavowable.

The fact that this use is much more common in literature than in cin-ema or in the various possible sorts of pornographic spectacle (at least, that is this author's conjecture on the basis of limited experience) surely has to do with technical difficulties (the demands of acting, sound record-ing, etc.), but it also has to do with the fact that sexual exclamations can be considered a sort of poetry *in nuce* just as easily as they can be regarded as a pornographic image of the second degree, doubling vision on the plane of language.

In effect, the exclamation—above all in the somewhat paradigmatic form of "I'm coming!" or even "Fuck! I can't go on . . .!" not to mention "Yes!" (think of the last line of Joyce's *Ulysses*)—in this form, the essence of which is gathered in the assonant French phrase *oui, je (tu) jouis!* ["Yes, I am (you are) coming!"], utters nothing but an obvious fact. It expresses what is taking place and what has no need of being announced. It is a tautology in action, for which the use of language offers few equivalents (if not, perhaps, the complaint "I'm sick . . .," but this expression can also, and more easily, transmit a piece of information).

This use of speech refers simultaneously to tautology (or, rather, "tautegory," the word Schelling uses in talking about myth) and to performativity. Everything happens as if "I am (you are) coming" effectively made one come, or at least as if the statement was itself a part of coming, and as if, as a result, coming was saying or being said, just as much as saying, and "the" saying (saying "that") was coming. At which point we would also have to try to understand that "the saying," itself and absolutely, is jouissance.

In the same way we must come to understand that designating certain things (gestures, parts of the body, tastes . . .) obscene and "shameful" is a desperate attempt to reach the hidden heart of jouissance, to show its eclipse. "Despair" here has to do with knowledge of the impossible, but at the same time it carries us beyond this overly simple designation: "impossible." After all, it designates and gives form to possibility itself. This is also why, if pornography consists in remaining attached to the fantasy of exhibition (and to the exclamation as overexhibition), love (or whatever we want to call it), by contrast, leaves fantasy behind and withdraws from the cry into murmur and silence.

Exclamation then touches the center of the pornographic enigma. On the one hand, it says nothing. It doubles the act with an act of supposed naming (as if "fuck!" could name what happens . . .). But, on the other hand, it is really only one more thrust of the act itself. For there is in fact nothing to say or show. This is the impasse that constitutes pornography. At the same time, this impasse is said, whether in the non-said that is nevertheless exclaimed or in the poorly said, the "blasphemy" and "imprecation" that link the exclamation less to religious transgression than to the anger unleashed against itself by speech run wild, at the very point when it can say only too much or too little. It could then be pointed out to Lacan that, if sexual relation "cannot be written" (which is to say, if there is no "report" [*rapport*] of it, no consigned and signifying relation), it is said, and is said up to, or maybe starting from, the extremity of its exclamation.

৵

I've cited a passage from *Everything Is Illuminated* here. But that, like the last page of *Ulysses*, is only one out of a million other possible references to literature. It is not by accident that this is the true place where the exclamation can be given a word that is capable of carrying it, for a moment. This is why a complete literary bibliography is in principle impossible here. It is better, therefore, to forego a bibliography in favor of just citing Apollinaire. This is from one of his *Poèmes à Madeleine*:

> This is what the symphonic song of love heard in the conch shell of
>   Venus is made of
> There is the song of the love of times gone by
> The sound of the frantic kisses of famous lovers
> The love-cries of mortal women raped by gods
> The male members of fabled heroes erect as church candles come and
>   go like an obscene murmur
> There are also the demented cries of Bacchantes mad with love from
>   eating the hippomane secreted by the vulvas of mares in heat
> The love-cries of felines in the jungle
> The dull sound of sap rising in tropical plants
> The racket of the tides
> The thunder of artillery batteries' obscenely shaped cannons enacting
>   the terrible love of peoples
> The waves of the sea birthplace of life and beauty
> And the song of victory that the first rays of sunshine caused Memnon
>   the unmoving to sing
> There is the cry of the Sabines at the moment of their ravishment
> The wedding song of the Sulamite
> I am black but beautiful
> And Jason's priceless cry
> At finding the Fleece
> And the swan's mortal song as its down pressed between Leda's blue-
>   white thighs
> There is the song of all the love in the world
> Between your beloved thighs Madeleine
> The murmur of all love just as the sacred song of the entire ocean
>   sounds in the seashell[6]

Notes

The "There Is" of Sexual Relation

1. [The English word *relation* is used to translate the French *rapport* throughout, with rare exceptions: when *relation* is used to translate the French word *relation*, the French is included in square brackets, and when the author makes a point of distinguishing the French words *relation* and *rapport*, the French is included in square brackets in both cases.—Trans.]

2. The first occasion for which this piece was prepared was an address delivered at the invitation of the École lacanienne de psychanalyse to mark the centennial of the birth of Lacan on May 6, 2001. Guy Le Gauffey and Georges-Henri Melenotte presided over the meeting, whose theme was "There is no sexual relation." The final version of the text is indebted to certain contributions to the discussion that followed the lecture. I am grateful to all the participants. I am also grateful to the seminar of the Instituto italiano per i studi filosofici di Venezia, where the lecture was also delivered in June 2001.

3. [Throughout this paragraph, the English word *relation* translates the French word *relation*, not *rapport*.—Trans.]

4. Guy Le Gauffrey has suggested that I say that *sexual relation* might very well be a redundancy.

5. G. W. F. Hegel, *Encyclopedia*, addition to section 97.

6. Derrida's *différance* must therefore be sexual. That is to say, ontological difference is sexual (and vice versa, which no doubt affects being in its very being-ness [*étance ou estance*]. Therefore being is sexed and/or sexing. (See at least "*Geschlecht*" in *Psyché* (Paris: Galilée, 1987) [published in English as "*Geschlecht* I: Sexual Difference, Ontological Difference," in *Psyche: Inventions of the Other*, ed. Peggy Kamuf and Elizabeth G. Rottenberg (Stanford, Calif.: Stanford

University Press, 2008), 7–27]). And so too the "god" (male or female?) of the ontotheological constitution of metaphysics, who is thereby engaged in a sexuating self-destruction. The distinctive complexity of the sexual and erotic mystery of Christianity (all the way from the Virgin Mary to the sinful flesh, passing through mystical union along the way) needs to be revisited starting from this point.

7. The Biblical usage has made us all familiar with the fact that Semitic languages use the verbs meaning *to know* to indicate the sexual relation.

8. René Descartes, *The Passions of the Soul*, article 137, in *The Philosophical Writings of Descartes*, ed. John Cottingham, Robert Stoothoff, and Dugald Murdoch (Cambridge: Cambridge University Press, 1985), 376.

9. More broadly, what is called for here is a whole analysis of the *Symposium* and the *Phaedrus*, an analysis that needs to be redone with and after Lacan, among others.

10. David Hume, *Treatise of Human Nature*, ed. Ernest Campbell Mossner (London: Penguin, 1984), bk. 2, pt. 2, § 9, and bk. 33, pt. 3, § 3; the references are to pp. 444, 441, and 432, 627, and 766, respectively.

11. [". . . der Kuß, nächtlich,/brennt einer Sprache den Sinn ein. . . ." Paul Celan, *Gedichte in Zwei Banden* (Frankfurt am Main: Suhrkamp, 1991), 290.—Trans.]

12. This was suggested to me by Chantal Klein, who also pointed out a certain analogy between this whole logic of sex and the one Nicolas Abraham deals with in *L'écorce et le noyau* (Paris: Flammarion, 1996). In fact—though this is not the place to stop to investigate it—the consequences of this would be analogous for Oedipus, operating not so much on the incest taboo as on any access to sexuality at all.

13. Norman Mailer, *Genius and Lust: A Journey Through the Major Writings of Henry Miller* (New York: Grove, 1976), 92.

The Birth of Breasts

1. Gustave Flaubert, *Mémoires d'un fou*, in *Oeuvres* (Paris: Flammarion, 1991), 9:304. "Diary of a Madman," in *Early Writings*, trans. Robert Griffin (Lincoln: University of Nebraska Press, 1991), 189.

2. Unica Zurn, "Das Haus der Krankheiten," in *Gesamtausgabe* (Berlin: Brinkmann & Bose, 1991), 4.1:66.

3. Yves Bonnefoy, *Dans le leurre du seuil* (Paris: Mercure de France, 1975), 24.

4. Jean-Christophe Bailly, "Théâtre et Agora," in *Prendre place: Espace public et culture dramatique*, ed. Isaac Joseph (Paris: Recherches, 1995), 51.

5. Max Jacob, *The Dice Cup: Selected Prose Poems*, trans. Michael Brownstein (New York: Sun, 1979), 45.

6. Monique Brossard-Le Grand, *Le sein ou la vie des femmes* (Paris: Renaudot, 1989), 159.

7. Jean-Jacques Rousseau, *Julie; or, the New Heloise*, trans. Philip Stewart and Jean Vaché (Hanover, N.H.: University Press of New England, 1997), pt. 2, 21, p. 218.

8. Novalis, *Notes for a Romantic Encyclopaedia: Das Allgemeine Brouillon*, trans., ed., and introd. David W. Wood (Albany: State University of New York Press, 2007), 42.

9. Paul Celan, "La Contrescarpe," in *Die Niemandsrose* (Frankfurt am Main: Fischer, 1963), 83.

10. Joseph Kessel, *Dames de Californie* (Paris: Gallimard, 1996), 16.

11. Friedrich Hölderlin, "The Rhine," in *Poems and Fragments*, trans. Michael Hamburger (London: Anvil, 1994), 433.

12. Giorgos Seferis, "Haiku" (1929), translated into French by Xavier Bordes and Robert Longueville, *Poésie* 40 (1987). [Translated from the French.—Trans.]

13. Valery Larbaud, "Beauté, mon beau souci . . .," *Amants, heureux amants*, in *Oeuvres* (Paris: Gallimard, 1957), 570.

14. Homer, *Iliad*, trans. Rodney Merrill (Ann Arbor: University of Michigan Press, 2007), 14:214–220, p. 254.

15. Pascal Quignard, *Vie secrète* (Paris: Gallimard, 1998), 30.

16. Henri Michaux, *A Barbarian in Asia*, trans. Sylvia Beach (New York: New Directions, 1949), 179–80.

17. Pierre de Ronsard, "Elégie à Janet, peintre du roi," in *Les Amours*, (Paris: Audin, 1949), 1:99.

18. Stéphane Mallarmé, "Monologue d'un faun," in *Oeuvres complètes* (Paris: Gallimard, 1998), 1:153.

19. Paul Valéry, *La jeune parque*, trans. Alistair Elliot (Newcastle upon Tyne: Bloodaxe, 1997), 19.

20. Jacques Lacan, Seminar VIII, in *Le Transfert* (Paris: Seuil, 1991), 444.

21. Jean-Claude Milner, "Retour à Saussure," in *Lettres sur tous les sujets, Le Perroquet*, no. 12, April 1994, pp. 14–15.

22. [*Seing* is also translated as *signature* and refers to the signature on a document verifying its authenticity.—Trans.]

23. Jacques Derrida, *Glas*, trans. John P. Leavey, Jr., and Richard Rand (Lincoln: University of Nebraska Press, 1986), 32–33.

24. Jacques Derrida, "Aletheia," in *"Nous avons voué notre vie à des signes"* (Paris: William Blake and Company, 1996).

25. Matthieu Bénézet, *Ode à la poésie* (Paris: William Blake and Company, 1992), 26.

26. Marcel Proust, *Sodom and Gomorrah, In Search of Lost Time*, trans. C. K. Scott Moncrieff and Terence Kilmartin, rev. by D. J. Enright (New York: The Modern Library, 1993), 4:263. Thanks to Mary Rawlinson for her help in finding this passage.

27. Sigmund Freud, posthumous note, *Gesammelte Werke*, ed. Anna Freud et al. (London: Imago, 1940–68), 18:152. Philip Roth has written a book, *The*

Breast, (New York: Holt, Rinehart and Winston, 1972), in which the narrator/ hero is a man who has turned into a breast.

28. Richard Yates, *Eleven Kinds of Loneliness* (New York: Little, Brown, 1962), 37.

29. Ezra Pound, "A Draft of XXX Cantos," in *The Cantos of Ezra Pound* (New York: New Directions, 1970), 11.

30. Michel Deguy, "Figurations," in *Poèmes, 1960–1970* (Paris: Gallimard, 1973), 117.

31. Maurice Blanchot, *Thomas the Obscure*, trans. Robert Lamberton (Barry-town, N.Y.: Station Hill Press, 1973), 84.

32. Auguste Renoir, cited in *Pierre-Auguste Renoir, Painter*, a film by Michael Gaummitz, produced by La Cinquième/Lapsus/RMN/Arion Média, 1999.

33. Christa Wolf, *Patterns of Childhood*, formerly published as *A Model Childhood*, trans. Ursule Molinaro and Hedwig Rappolt (New York: Farrar, Straus and Giroux, 1984), 287. The work originally appeared in German as *Kindheitsmuster* (Berlin: Aufbau, 1976).

34. Ginevra Bompiani, *The Great Bear*, trans. Brian Kern and Sergio Parussa (New York: Italica, 2000), 52–54.

35. Friedrich Nietzsche, writing about Lou Salomé, draft of a letter to Georg Rée, brother of Paul Rée, Letter 435 in *Briefe 6* in *Sämtliche Briefe* (Berlin: W. de Gruyter, 1986), 402.

36. Fernando Pessoa, "Epithalamium," in *Poemas Ingleses* (Lisbon: Ediçoes Ática, 1974), 128.

37. Françoise Cledat, *La chambre de mon fils* (Paris: Tarabuste, 2004), 19.

38. Gilles Deleuze/Felix Guattari, *A Thousand Plateaus: Capitalism and Schizophrenia*, trans. Brian Massumi (Minneapolis: University of Minnesota Press, 1987), 61–62.

39. Rousseau, *Julie*, pt. 2, 22, p. 229.

40. Valéry, *La jeune parque*, 21, 25.

41. Aristotle, *The Parts of Animals*, trans. A. L. Peck (Cambridge: Harvard University Press, 1961), 688a. Trans. modified.

42. Leonidas of Tarentum, in *The Poems of Leonid of Tarentum*, trans. Edwyn Bevan (Oxford: Oxford University Press, 1931), 20.

43. Friedrich Hölderlin, "Der Wanderer," in *Sämtliche Werke* (Stuttgart: Kohlhammer, 1955), 2:84–85.

44. Valéry, *La jeune parque*, 33.

45. Henry Miller, *Opus pistorum* (New York: Grove, 1983), 199.

46. Guy de Maupassant, "Yvette," in *Yvette and Ten Other Stories*, trans. Mrs. John Galsworthy (New York: Knopf, 1915), 15—20. Trans. modified.

47. Daniela Battini, "Personne, l'autre." Unpublished.

48. Gustave Flaubert, "Diary of a Madman," in *Early Writings*, trans. Robert Griffin (Lincoln: University of Nebraska Press, 1991), 180.

49. William Shakespeare, *The Merchant of Venice*, 4.1.316–17.

50. Claude Simon, *Histoire*, trans. Richard Howard (New York: Braziller, 1968), 341.

51. *Jamón, Jamón*, a film by Bigas Luna. Lolafilms, S.A./Ovídeo TV S.A./ Sogepaq, 1992. The French text quotes the French subtitled version of the film; the translation is from the French.

52. Françoise Ducout, *Greta Garbo la somnambule* (Paris: Stock, 1979).

53. Catherine Weinzaepflen, *Totem* (Paris: Flammarion, 1985), 97.

54. Agrippa d'Aubigné, *Les tragiques*, in *Oeuvres VIII, 1203–1208* (Paris: Gallimard, 1969), 243.

55. James Joyce, *Ulysses* (London: The Bodley Head, 1960), 933.

56. F. A. de Chateaubriand, *The Martyrs* (New York: Whiting and Watson, 1812), 2:48.

57. Clement Marot, "Of the Fair Breast," in *Lyrics of the French Renaissance*, trans. Norman Shapiro (New Haven, Conn.: Yale University Press, 2002), 99.

58. Mercier de Compiègne, *Éloge du sein des femmes* (Paris: Barraud, 1873).

59. Ramón Gomez de la Serna, *Senos* (Madrid: Prodhufi, 1992), 34–36. Translated by Lori Gallegos de Castillo.

60. Italo Calvino, *Under the Jaguar Sun*, trans. William Weaver (London: Jonathan Cape, 1992), 75.

61. James Joyce, *Finnegans Wake* (London: Faber and Faber, 1975), 215.

62. Hermann Broch, *The Death of Virgil*, trans. Jean Starr Untermeyer (New York: Pantheon, 1945), 297.

63. Avital Ronell, *The Telephone Book* (Lincoln: University of Nebraska Press, 1989), 337–40.

64. *The Texts of Early Greek Philosophy: The Complete Fragments and Selected Testimonies of the Major Presocratics*, part I, trans. and ed. Daniel W. Graham (Cambridge: Cambridge University Press, 2010), 567.

65. Derrida, *Glas*, 114.

66. Joyce, *Ulysses*, 892.

67. Mirabeau, *Le libertin de qualité; ou, Ma conversion* (Paris: Euredif, 1976), 67.

68. Joyce Carol Oates, "Pinch," in *The Assignation* (New York: Ecco, 1988), 66.

69. [In this extended quotation, Nancy translates Lipps's *Gefühl* and the verb *fühlen* using the French terms *sentiment* and *sentir*, respectively. In the English I have used both *sentiment* and *sense* for *Gefühl*, depending on context, and *to sense* for *fühlen*.—Trans.]

70. Theodor Lipps, *Grundlegung der Aesthetik* (Leipzig: Leopold Voss, 1903), 1:147–51. [My thanks to Michael Popowits for his help in translating this passage.—Trans.]

71. François Truffaut, *Domicile conjugal* (Paris: Les Films du Carosse Films , 1970).

72. Samuel Beckett, *Watt* (New York: Grove, 1970), 108–9.

73. Mallarmé, "Le phénomene futur," in *Poèmes en prose*, in *Oeuvres complètes*, 1:413.

74. Maupassant, "Yvette," in *Yvette and Ten Other Stories*, 54–55.

75. Ezra Pound, "The Pisan Cantos," in *The Cantos of Ezra Pound*, 487.

76. Agrippa d'Aubigné, *Odes*, no. 23 in *Oeuvres* (Paris: Gallimard, 1969), 314.

77. Claude Simon, *The Acacia*, trans. Richard Howard (New York: Pantheon, 1991), 276.

78. Jacques Lacan, *The Four Fundamental Concepts of Psychoanalysis*, trans. Alan Sheridan (Norton: New York, 1998), 195.

79. Theophile Gautier, *Arria Marcella*, in *Oeuvres* (Paris: Lemerre, 1898), 1:331.

80. Chateaubriand, *The Martyrs*, 3:259.

81. Georges Bataille, "L'archangélique," in *Oeuvres complètes* (Paris: Gallimard, 1971), 3:88.

82. Antonin Artaud, *Suppots et supplications*, in *Oeuvres complètes* (Paris: Gallimard, 1978), 14:19.

83. Sappho, *Sappho*, trans. Renée Vivien (Paris: Lemerre, 1902), 31. [Translated from the French.—Trans.]

84. Novalis, *L'encyclopédie*, translated into French by Maurice de Gandillac (Paris: Minuit, 1966), 236. [Translated from French.—Trans.]

85. Song of Solomon 8:10.

86. G. W. F. Hegel, *The Phenomenology of Spirit*, trans. A. V. Miller (Oxford: Oxford University Press, 1977), para. 87, p. 56.

87. Malcolm Lowry, *Under the Volcano* (London: Penguin, 1962), 91–92.

88. Marcel Proust, *Within a Budding Grove, In Search of Lost Time*, 2:337.

89. Samuel Beckett, "Enough," in *First Love and Other Shorts* (New York: Grove, 1974), 60.

90. Friedrich Hölderlin, "And to experience . . . ," in *Hymns and Fragments*, trans. Richard Sieburth (Princeton: Princeton University Press, 1984), 195.

There Is Sexual Relation—and Then

1. .[*Sex appeal* is in English in the original.—Trans.]

2. After the seminar I read the article "Exclamations," which I put together on this subject for the *Dictionnaire de la pornographie* (Paris: Presses Universitaires de France, 2005). I have added the text of that entry here as an appendix.

3. Marquis de Sade, *Les prospérités du vice* (Paris: UGE, 1969), 171.

4. See Christian Prigent, "Un gros fil rouge ciré," in *L'intenable* (Paris: P.O.L., 2004).

5. Jonathan Safran Foer, *Everything Is Illuminated* (Boston: Houghton Mifflin, 2003).

6. Guillame Apollinaire, *Letters to Madeleine*, ed. Laurence Campa, trans. Donald Nicholson-Smith (London: Seagull, 2010), 471–72.

Perspectives in Continental Philosophy

John D. Caputo, series editor

Karl Jaspers, *The Question of German Guilt*. Introduction by Joseph W. Koterski, S.J.

Jean-Luc Marion, *The Idol and Distance: Five Studies*. Translated with an introduction by Thomas A. Carlson.

Jeffrey Dudiak, *The Intrigue of Ethics: A Reading of the Idea of Discourse in the Thought of Emmanuel Levinas*.

Robyn Horner, *Rethinking God as Gift: Marion, Derrida, and the Limits of Phenomenology*.

Mark Dooley, *The Politics of Exodus: Søren Kierkegaard's Ethics of Responsibility*.

Merold Westphal, *Overcoming Onto-Theology: Toward a Postmodern Christian Faith*.

Edith Wyschogrod, Jean-Joseph Goux, and Eric Boynton, eds., *The Enigma of Gift and Sacrifice*.

Stanislas Breton, *The Word and the Cross*. Translated with an introduction by Jacquelyn Porter.

Jean-Luc Marion, *Prolegomena to Charity*. Translated by Stephen E. Lewis.

Peter H. Spader, *Scheler's Ethical Personalism: Its Logic, Development, and Promise*.

Jean-Louis Chrétien, *The Unforgettable and the Unhoped For*. Translated by Jeffrey Bloechl.

Don Cupitt, *Is Nothing Sacred? The Non-Realist Philosophy of Religion: Selected Essays*.

Jean-Luc Marion, *In Excess: Studies of Saturated Phenomena*. Translated by Robyn Horner and Vincent Berraud.

Phillip Goodchild, *Rethinking Philosophy of Religion: Approaches from Continental Philosophy*.

William J. Richardson, S.J., *Heidegger: Through Phenomenology to Thought*.

Jeffrey Andrew Barash, *Martin Heidegger and the Problem of Historical Meaning*.

Jean-Louis Chrétien, *Hand to Hand: Listening to the Work of Art*. Translated by Stephen E. Lewis.

Jean-Louis Chrétien, *The Call and the Response*. Translated with an introduction by Anne Davenport.

D. C. Schindler, *Han Urs von Balthasar and the Dramatic Structure of Truth: A Philosophical Investigation*.

Julian Wolfreys, ed., *Thinking Difference: Critics in Conversation*.

Allen Scult, *Being Jewish/Reading Heidegger: An Ontological Encounter*.

Richard Kearney, *Debates in Continental Philosophy: Conversations with Contemporary Thinkers*.

Jennifer Anna Gosetti-Ferencei, *Heidegger, Hölderlin, and the Subject of Poetic Language: Toward a New Poetics of Dasein*.

Jolita Pons, *Stealing a Gift: Kierkegaard's Pseudonyms and the Bible*.

Jean-Yves Lacoste, *Experience and the Absolute: Disputed Questions on the Humanity of Man*. Translated by Mark Raftery-Skehan.

Charles P. Bigger, *Between* Chora *and the* Good: *Metaphor's Metaphysical Neighborhood*.

Dominique Janicaud, *Phenomenology "Wide Open": After the French Debate.* Translated by Charles N. Cabral.

Ian Leask and Eoin Cassidy, eds., *Givenness and God: Questions of Jean-Luc Marion.*

Jacques Derrida, *Sovereignties in Question: The Poetics of Paul Celan.* Edited by Thomas Dutoit and Outi Pasanen.

William Desmond, *Is There a Sabbath for Thought? Between Religion and Philosophy.*

Bruce Ellis Benson and Norman Wirzba, eds., *The Phenomenology of Prayer.*

S. Clark Buckner and Matthew Statler, eds., *Styles of Piety: Practicing Philosophy after the Death of God.*

Kevin Hart and Barbara Wall, eds., *The Experience of God: A Postmodern Response.*

John Panteleimon Manoussakis, *After God: Richard Kearney and the Religious Turn in Continental Philosophy.*

John Martis, *Philippe Lacoue-Labarthe: Representation and the Loss of the Subject.*

Jean-Luc Nancy, *The Ground of the Image.*

Edith Wyschogrod, *Crossover Queries: Dwelling with Negatives, Embodying Philosophy's Others.*

Gerald Bruns, *On the Anarchy of Poetry and Philosophy: A Guide for the Unruly.*

Brian Treanor, *Aspects of Alterity: Levinas, Marcel, and the Contemporary Debate.*

Simon Morgan Wortham, *Counter-Institutions: Jacques Derrida and the Question of the University.*

Leonard Lawlor, *The Implications of Immanence: Toward a New Concept of Life.*

Clayton Crockett, *Interstices of the Sublime: Theology and Psychoanalytic Theory.*

Bettina Bergo, Joseph Cohen, and Raphael Zagury-Orly, eds., *Judeities: Questions for Jacques Derrida.* Translated by Bettina Bergo and Michael B. Smith.

Jean-Luc Marion, *On the Ego and on God: Further Cartesian Questions.* Translated by Christina M. Gschwandtner.

Jean-Luc Nancy, *Philosophical Chronicles.* Translated by Franson Manjali.

Jean-Luc Nancy, *Dis-Enclosure: The Deconstruction of Christianity.* Translated by Bettina Bergo, Gabriel Malenfant, and Michael B. Smith.

Andrea Hurst, *Derrida Vis-à-vis Lacan: Interweaving Deconstruction and Psychoanalysis.*

Jean-Luc Nancy, *Noli me tangere: On the Raising of the Body.* Translated by Sarah Clift, Pascale-Anne Brault, and Michael Naas.

Jacques Derrida, *The Animal That Therefore I Am.* Edited by Marie-Louise Mallet, translated by David Wills.

Jean-Luc Marion, *The Visible and the Revealed.* Translated by Christina M. Gschwandtner and others.

Michel Henry, *Material Phenomenology.* Translated by Scott Davidson.

Jean-Luc Nancy, *Corpus.* Translated by Richard A. Rand.

Joshua Kates, *Fielding Derrida.*

Michael Naas, *Derrida From Now On.*

Shannon Sullivan and Dennis J. Schmidt, eds., *Difficulties of Ethical Life.*

Catherine Malabou, *What Should We Do with Our Brain?* Translated by Sebastian Rand, Introduction by Marc Jeannerod.

Claude Romano, *Event and World*. Translated by Shane Mackinlay.

Vanessa Lemm, *Nietzsche's Animal Philosophy: Culture, Politics, and the Animality of the Human Being.*

B. Keith Putt, ed., *Gazing Through a Prism Darkly: Reflections on Merold Westphal's Hermeneutical Epistemology.*

Eric Boynton and Martin Kavka, eds., *Saintly Influence: Edith Wyschogrod and the Possibilities of Philosophy of Religion.*

Shane Mackinlay, *Interpreting Excess: Jean-Luc Marion, Saturated Phenomena, and Hermeneutics.*

Kevin Hart and Michael A. Signer, eds., *The Exorbitant: Emmanuel Levinas Between Jews and Christians.*

Bruce Ellis Benson and Norman Wirzba, eds., *Words of Life: New Theological Turns in French Phenomenology.*

William Robert, *Trials: Of Antigone and Jesus.*

Brian Treanor and Henry Isaac Venema, eds., *A Passion for the Possible: Thinking with Paul Ricoeur.*

Kas Saghafi, *Apparitions—Of Derrida's Other.*

Nick Mansfield, *The God Who Deconstructs Himself: Sovereignty and Subjectivity Between Freud, Bataille, and Derrida.*

Don Ihde, *Heidegger's Technologies: Postphenomenological Perspectives.*

Françoise Dastur, *Questioning Phenomenology*. Translated by Robert Vallier.

Suzi Adams, *Castoriadis's Ontology: Being and Creation.*

Richard Kearney and Kascha Semonovitch, eds., *Phenomenologies of the Stranger: Between Hostility and Hospitality.*

Michael Naas, *Miracle and Machine: Jacques Derrida and the Two Sources of Religion, Science, and the Media.*

Alena Alexandrova, Ignaas Devisch, Laurens ten Kate, and Aukje van Rooden, *Re-treating Religion: Deconstructing Christianity with Jean-Luc Nancy*. Preamble by Jean-Luc Nancy.

Emmanuel Falque, *The Metamorphosis of Finitude: An Essay on Birth and Resurrection*. Translated by George Hughes.

Scott M. Campbell, *The Early Heidegger's Philosophy of Life: Facticity, Being, and Language.*

Françoise Dastur, *How Are We to Confront Death? An Introduction to Philosophy*. Translated by Robert Vallier. Foreword by David Farrell Krell.

Christina M. Gschwandtner, *Postmodern Apologetics? Arguments for God in Contemporary Philosophy.*

Ben Morgan, *On Becoming God: Late Medieval Mysticism and the Modern Western Self.*

Neal DeRoo, *Futurity in Phenomenology: Promise and Method in Husserl, Levinas, and Derrida.*

Sarah LaChance Adams and Caroline R. Lundquist eds., *Coming to Life: Philosophies of Pregnancy, Childbirth, and Mothering.*

Thomas Claviez, ed., *The Conditions of Hospitality: Ethics, Politics, and Aesthetics on the Threshold of the Possible.*

Roland Faber and Jeremy Fackenthal, eds., *Theopoetic Folds: Philosophizing Multifariousness.*

Jean-Luc Marion, *The Essential Writings.* Edited by Kevin Hart.

Adam S. Miller, *Speculative Grace: Bruno Latour and Object-Oriented Theology.* Foreword by Levi R. Bryant

Jean-Luc Nancy, *Corpus II: Writings on Sexuality.*

David Nowell Smith, *Sounding/Silence: Martin Heidegger at the Limits of Poetics.*